Life's Too Short
for Anything but Love
and 101 other Musings, Essays, and Sundry Pieces

by

Robert Lee Hill

WOODNEATH PRESS

Kansas City

Published by Woodneath Press
8900 NE Flintlock Rd.
Kansas City, MO 64157

Cover design and typography by Cody Croan

Cover image photograph by Kim Horgan with permission for its use granted to the author.

Publisher's Cataloguing-in-Publication
(Provided by Woodneath Press: A Program of Mid-Continent Public Library)

Hill, Robert Lee
Life's Too Short For Anything But Love : And 101 other Musings, Essays, and Sundry Pieces / by Robert Lee Hill
p. cm.
LCCN
ISBN 978-1-942337-01-0

1.   Christian experience, practice, and life 2. Life -- Religious aspects – Christianity 3. Literary collections – Essays. I. Title.

248

Table of Contents

INTRODUCTION 1

VIEWS, OBSERVATIONS, & CELEBRATIONS OF
THE DAILY EXTRAORDINARY 3

Life's Too Short 5
A New Take on Old 7
"Altared" States of Being 9
Always Learning 11
C.H.U.R.C.H. 13
Church Family 15
Dear Jack 17
Commencements 20
Consecration 21
Democracy 23
F.O.R.G.I.V.E.N.E.S.S. 25
Holy Spirit 26
Home 28
Music is 30
Resurrection 31
Some New (Ironic) Takes on "Mercy" 33
Texts 35
What Churches Are For 37
Work 39

HIGH HOLY DAYS 41

All the Saints! 43
Thankful for Thanksgiving 44
Giving Thanks for Common Things 45
Advent and Christmas 47
Christmas Music 49
Some Items for a Christmas Gift List 51
Lent: A Many Splendored Season 52
Lent's ABCs 53
L.E.N.T. 55
8 Great Days of Holy Week 57
Holy Week Blessings Are Coming 59
EASTER - Remembrance, Reality, Resonance, Ray of
Hope 60

Easter Is Upon Us 64
Easter Is Here 66
Pentecost Is the Church's Way of Celebrating Its
Birthday 68

PRAYER **69**
In Praise of Prayer 71
Prayer at the Center 72
Prayers We Love to Pray 74
"Pray For Me" 75
A Prayer for July 4th 77
A Prayer Practice for Times When Prayer Is Hard 78
All Deaths Caused By Violence Are Tragic 79
Giving Thanks 81
Thankful for Dr. King's Prayers 83
Rejoicing and Weeping and Resurrection (+Resources
for Talking with Our Children About Tragedy) 84
Service of Unity and Hope 87

RESISTING HARMFUL RELIGION **91**
Resisting Harmful Religion 93
Living Faithfully, Beyond May 21, 2011 95
Letter re: Mr. Terry Jones 96
About Fred Phelps' Passing 98
About Osama bin Laden's Death 100

TRIBUTES, REMEMBRANCES, & APPRECIATIONS 103
Appreciations 105
Tribute for Judy Hellman at 2014 MORE² Banquet .106
Thomas Merton's Birthday 108
Thanks for Don Schutt 110
Thank You, Joseph Siry! Beth Sholom Congregation:
Frank Lloyd Wright and Modern Religious
Architecture 112
Thank You, Galway Kinnell 114
Thank You, B'nai Jehudah — Celebrating 75 years of
Congregational Friendship 115
Remembering K. David Cole 117
Remembering the Rev. Dr. William Sloane Coffin, Jr.,
April 13, 2006 119
Remembering Jack Sullivan 122
Remembering Denton Roberts 124
Remembering Dale Eldred 126
Remembering Forrest Church 128
Nelson Mandela, Thank You 131

Giving Thanks for Howard Thurman 133
Introduction and Tribute for Fred Craddock- July 11, 2011 134
A Nobel Prize for Wendell Berry 138
Famous Babies 139
Overcoming Great Odds 140
The Greatness of Gary Straub 142

TRUE TREASURES **145**
Treasure 147
The Challenge (and Centrality) of Superlatives 149
What's Your Undertone? 150
Some Contemporary Beatitudes 151
Whataburger Thanksgiving 152
Trip to Angola 155
The Wonders of Baseball 157
Steeple of Light 159
What I've Learned While at Community (After 10 Years) 161
The Teaching Tomatoes 163
The Religion on the Line Radio Show 164
The Biggest Little Word 167
Rowing 168
New Year's Resolutions 2014 170
Religion On the Line — Celebrating 20 Years On the Air! 172
Mother's Day 173
Mothers' Days 175
Rodin and "The Sufficiency of the Fragment" 176
Love on Valentine's Day 178
Leaves from The Notebook of A Tamed Optimist .. 180
Give Them, Give Them All, Give Them Now! 182
For the Beauty of the Earth 184
For Our Veterans on Veterans Day 186
First and Last Words 187
Famous 188
Ministry 190
Encountering God's Beautiful World Anew 192
Death's Sting 194
Back to the Garden 195
Always Building 197

A Wondrous and Happy Mess 199
You Are Welcome! 200
ACKNOWLEDGMENTS 201
ABOUT THE AUTHOR 202

INTRODUCTION

During my pastoral tenure at Community Christian Church in Kansas City, Missouri, I've enjoyed the privilege (and responsibility) of offering weekly commentary in Community's weekly newsletter, *The Community News*. Also across that same stretch of time, I've offered public statements at an array of civic and interfaith gatherings.

The weekly discipline of writing a church newsletter column has been a blessing to me, and, so some have reported, to a few others. Engaging in such a discipline has prodded me to think about, reflect upon, and shape an engagement with the world. Such newsletter columns are now quickly fading out of fashion. Blogs have taken their place, blogs being impressively more accessible and timely for a much broader readership.

On the other hand, a newsletter column — or any other writing task that rises out of a shared community — has the benefit of the particular place, relationships, and community which is the intended recipient for what one writes. Oftentimes, when I've tendered pastoral commentary, theological opinions, and reflective essays for *The Community News* and elsewhere, I've had a specific set of faces and lives in mind. At other times, I've imagined the congregation as a whole, friends, colleagues, and community groups as the intended audience.

Contained herein are a few of the more than 1,500 pieces I proffered to the grand congregation and friends of Community Christian Church. Also included are some public prayers, essays, and newspaper faith columns. They are collected here as a kind of valedictory gift to a community of faith, and to friends near and far, as I approach retirement from the senior minister position and receive the humbling title of "minister emeritus."

The topics and themes are wide-ranging and varied: celebrations of Wendell Berry, Howard Thurman, Thomas Merton, and precious friends whose exemplary lives have inspired me and countless others; musings on the blessings of baseball and a woman named "Treasure"; a Thanksgiving spent at Whataburger; an imagined letter to a Catholic friend; some commentaries about prayer; 22 years spent on the *Religion on the Line* radio call-in show; the necessity of resisting harmful religion; and exchanges with my friend "Seymour," who regularly dropped by my study at the church. Together they mark a place and a people and a pastor who had the blessed opportunity to share life together. That such markings will fade with the ravaging changes that attend history's incessant movement toward new life is undeniable and unavoidable. Whether any of these markings will endure as valuable only time will tell. For now these words recall, at least for a moment, three decades of cherished relationships, adventures, projects, books, dilemmas, challenges, ideas, hopes, and dreams. In the end perhaps it is enough for all to abide in a welcoming posture toward the future and for me simply to say "Thanks."

— Bob Hill
Brookside, Kansas City, Missouri

VIEWS, OBSERVATIONS, & CELEBRATIONS OF THE DAILY EXTRAORDINARY

Life's Too Short...

Ever since an existential speed bump at the tail end of a sabbatical journey, the precious nature of each new day has become progressively clear to me, and the miraculous character of each moment of earthly existence has been made increasingly plain. *Carpe Diem* (Latin for seize the day) is a grand motto to guide our steps, I believe.

The following selections from a recent cataloguing of reveries are offered to clarify some new and reinforced priority values.

Life's too short for instant coffee.
Life's too short for anything but honesty.
Life's too short for anything but wooden bats in baseball.
Life's too short to wallow in guilt.
Life's too short to hang onto a grudge.
Life's too short to ignore autumn leaves.
Life's too short for not forgiving others.
Life's too short to be a victim.
Life's too short to disregard even one full moon.
Life's too short not to have poetry in your life.
Life's too short not to play with your grandchildren.
Life's too short to forget your sister's birthday.
Life's too short for processed cheese.
Life's too short not to have a favorite color.
Life's too short not to grill out every chance you can.
Life's too short to live without courtesy.
Life's too short not to pet a cat whose back rises to your touch.
Life's too short to be cynical for even a nanosecond.
Life's too short for bad manners.
Life's too short to ignore a snow rainbow.
Life's too short not to savor a peach.
Life's too short to be a coward.
Life's too short not to stand up for justice for all people.
Life's too short not to exercise your citizenship on Election Day.
Life's too short to color with only four crayons in your 64-crayon pack.
Life's too short not to make new friends.
Life's too short not to pray.
Life's too short to be cheap.
Life's too short not to learn how to enjoy a new kind of music once a year.

Life's too short for anything but 15% tips.
Life's too short to refuse a hug.
Life's too short to neglect your birthday.
Life's too short to show anything but respect for our elders.
Life's too short to show anything but kindness toward a stranger.
Life's too short to be unmerciful.
Life's too short to be stingy.
Life's too short to be ungrateful for each new day.
Life's too short for anything but love.

A New Take on Old

I've been thinking this week about the concept of "old." I don't think I'll go as far as Marilynne Robinson does in suggesting a complete rehabilitation for the word "old." But it's good to note how "old" has both positive and pejorative meanings.

"Old school," depending on the context, can mean stodgy, or it can mean strong and trustworthy. "Grow old along with me," said Robert Browning, championing the achievement of oldness as a good thing and something to be shared. On the other hand, "I don't want just to be old," said a friend as she expressed anxiety about merely increasing in years without increasing in wisdom or insight.

There are some things in life that are simply "old" — meaning outdated, past their prime, beyond usefulness, maybe even harmful. Think of the use of medieval pillories for punishment. Or the practice of imposing poll taxes for the right of voting. Or relying on sundials to tell time in your car. (Which is not only "old" but rather ridiculously impossible.) Or bloodletting to cure physical maladies.

But there are also incomparable blessings that come with being old. This year our house is 100 years old. In 1912 the Kansas City Water Department issued a permit that allowed the water to be turned on in our home, which was apparently at the southernmost extension of the Brookside neighborhood at that time. The water has been available and the house occupied ever since. For 100 years, our home has been a dwelling place of shelter and grace and comfort. Think of it! 100 years "old" — meaning seasoned, lived in, appreciated, treasured, improved upon, added to, cared for, enjoyed.

On the other hand, if we compare any of our homes in the United States (even the oldest timber frame house in the U.S., the Fairbanks House in Dedham, Massachusetts, circa 1637) with some of the dwelling places in Europe, ours are mere youngsters, pipsqueaks, hardly old at all.

Once, on a visit to the ruins of Ephesus, someone reminded our tour group that the marbled streets there are at least 2,300 years old. "Whew," I thought, "now that's *old!*" I was glad those streets were there, and I sought to listen to the stories they could tell, stories about "the old days," but also stories with gifts as fresh as a new day's sun.

This week I'm abiding in a refreshing combination of appreciations. I'm glad for the oldness of the earth and for time-tested faith disciplines like prayer and worship and ancient songs that are seemingly "as old as the hills." And I am gleefully glad, as happy as a kindergartner, that there are immense aspects of the human journey that "never grow old." Like walking on a new or an old path, and laughing with new and old friends, and taking new ways home to our old house.

In short, to quote an "old adage," "There's old, and then there's old."

"Altared" States of Being

There are altars in every religion. Some are made of stone. Some are made of wood. Some are made of metal. Some are made of glass. Some are square. Some are rectangular. Some are round. Sometimes altars are high and lifted up. Sometimes they are situated deep within the recesses of a worship space. Sometimes they're right in the middle of a sanctuary. But wherever we go, in whatever religious space we find ourselves, there is an altar.

The word "altar" means "place of sacrifice or ritual practice." In ancient times, some altars were bloodied by the ritual sacrifices of animals. Such practice was deemed necessary for pleasing and enjoying right relationship with a deity. Since the nearly universal abolishment of such bloody rites, sacrifice has come to have spiritual and symbolic meanings.

In the Christian tradition, there has been a strong, if not ubiquitous, reference to Christ as offering his life as a sacrifice for humanity's sins. In all cases, both then and now, an altar signifies an arresting reality: "This is a place where we remember the presence of the holy."

In Christian liturgy, founded on Judaism's observance of worship at an altar as portrayed in the Old Testament, an altar was regularly placed at one extremity of a sanctuary, with the worship leader facing east. (By the way, since the destruction of the second temple in the year 70 CE, Judaism has foregone the use of an altar and instead has observed the veneration of an "ark" in which sacred Torah scrolls are placed.)

For Protestant Christians, particularly those in the Reformed and Free Church traditions, the communion table has become a central focus of attention, but it functions in much the same way as an altar functions for Catholic Christians: here we renew our remembrance of the blessed presence of God.

Now altars can be both intimidating and alluring. For some folks, an altar may seem unwelcoming: "After all, who am I to dare to approach the Holy? I've been told that only 'special people' are permitted at the altar? Am I that 'special'? Can I really be accepted by God?" For others, an altar is the best place to be: "Here I know once again that I am accepted, just as I am!

Here everyone is welcome, including me, and this is cause for celebration! I'm glad for this physical reminder of spiritual grace!"

For one and all, particularly for Christians, an altar, by whatever name we call it, signifies our human inclination toward "altared" states of being. In a wedding we lead our beloved to the altar of commitment and devotion. At prayer times we lay our confessions, petitions, and thanksgiving before the altar of God's grace. In the midst of worship, we surround the altar of celebration with our praises.

We are the religious animal who speaks of God and ourselves in the same breath. We can do no other. Our quest to be altered, that is, transformed, into better conformity with the Imago Dei (image of God) in which we were created, happens best when we are "altared," that is, graced, by wondrous reminders of the presence of God in all aspects of our lives.

Always Learning

Every year at Community we celebrate our graduates during worship. Far from being simply an annual rite of passage, this is an occasion for us to highlight the hard work, study, and attainments of the students among us, both high school and college.

Our graduation celebrations also highlight a transition for our graduates from institutional learning to lifelong learning. Educational institutions, when they fulfill their highest calling, do not merely prepare students for better jobs, or career advancement, or the establishment of a stable financial foundation. When educators truly educate, they teach us how to learn. May we always know and know always anew the multiple meanings of learning.

Learning is the expansion of a child's heart as well as her mind. Learning is a young one fashioning dreams, and an old one sharing visions. If we pay attention, learning is what takes place when knees are skinned, egos are bruised, and souls are stretched by new awareness.

Learning is to knowledge what burning is to fire. Learning is the beginning of new life and the closing off of that which has passed the point of usefulness. To learn is to encounter every present moment as a potential blessing.

Learning is an adventure in uncharted territory. It is the challenge of all good managers, all insightful inventors, all masterful musicians, all wonderstruck painters, and all worthy teachers.

Learning takes place by staying awake, paying attention, and doing your homework. Learning also happens by simply sitting on the edge of a peacefully gleaming lake, or watching clouds pass by overhead, or listening to the gentle rhythms of rain. Learning is not kept under lock and key at the schoolhouse.

Learning is essential for every effort toward quality, and it is unavoidable in the natural scheme of maturation. Either we learn or we wither. Learning inspires the mind and checks our brazenness. Learning humbles the highest and ennobles the lowly.

Learning is the breaking of poverty's shackles. It is an escape hatch out of the pit of prejudice. It is the living link which draws disparate groups together. Without learning, history moves in retrograde; with learning, we take the next authentic step into the future.

Learning shines on a graduates face. Learning empowers the disenfranchised and lifts up the downtrodden. Learning is the great democratizer. Learning is the ultimate check-and-balance system. It is the stimulus for all virtues and the corrective for all vices.

C.H.U.R.C.H.

There are always encouraging constants which we, as members of Christ's great Church, can rely upon as our "job definition." Qualities such as the following surely are part of what it means to be a Church in our day and time:

Compassion — The Church is always to bear compassion within itself and outward toward others. The cup of cold water to the thirsty person is not merely an act of out-of-date piety; it is a duty in response to the call of God to love our neighbors as ourselves.

Hospitality — The Church probably should teach courses on hospitality, since that should be one of the hallmarks of our attitudes and actions toward all people. Little children, big children, the stranger, the friend, the newcomer in the neighborhood, the person of longstanding service, the down-and-out, the up-and-coming, the poor, the wealthy, the hale and healthy, the shattered and battered — all these are to receive the best hospitality we can muster.

Understanding — Let us never forget that the faith which Jesus promoted was and is one of understanding, not only sympathy for another's position but rigorous exploring and discovery of new truths as they develop. This means reason always has a place in the Christian life. We are to recall that "Jesus came to wipe away our sins, not our minds."

Resurrection — In the midst of a world so desperately in need of new life, rejuvenation, and a fresh spirit, nothing seems so important as the proclamation that resurrection is possible. In the revived commitment in parents yearning to be and do their best; the resuscitated dreams of a student who has overcome a failure; in the revitalized aspirations of a worker on a brand-new job; in the flurry of activity of an author who has endured a long dry spell of writer's block; in the proud plowing of a farmer after a definitive break in a drought; in the sobriety of a person who has known the destructiveness of addiction: indeed, resurrection can be and is possible everywhere.

Challenge — To be in the Church is to engage in a consistent response to the moral and ethical challenges of our lives. The faith to which Christ calls all followers is no tepid feeling of accommodation. Rather it is a challenge to be "in the world but not of the world." In short, many times it is not easy to be a Christian.

Hope — There is possibly nothing so direly needed as the experience of hope in people's lives. In a culture that overly prides itself in perfectionism, people often feel like failures. In a culture which celebrates "hyper-individualism," people feel hopelessly isolated. Yet the Church, possibly more effectively than any other institution, can and does lift up hopefulness and the empowerment which hoping can bring to the human community. To abide in hope is to remember that God's ways of love and truth always have the last word.

Church Family

In more ways than we know, a congregation is a family of families. Of all the images and ideal pictures of the Church, "a family of faith" is surely among our favorites. And who is not stirred by the humbly powerful imagery of "the Holy Family" at Christmastime? Within the wider reaches of the ecclesial family, we often picture our sojourner Christians as "brothers and sisters in Christ." In olden days, familial language was so indelibly ingrained that church members were often referred to as "Brother Smith" and "Sister Jones." Sometimes such language seemed stilted and superficial. But at other times, such terms of endearment were truly the lexicon of love for the new creation which was headed up by Christ.

In the first century Church, some of the most memorable terminology for Christian companions included the reference "the church in your house," with all of its family overtones. The Apostle Paul frequently implored his distant compatriots to welcome his visiting friends and emissaries into their hearts and homes, as if they all were just one big cantankerous family. And we can never forget that Peter and Paul also were enraged and discombobulated about the vagaries and variances of their troops, just like family members get energized, exasperated and obviously bothered when certain actions and attitudes prevail to the detriment of the household of all concerned. And, on the other hand, as our "Dinners for Eight" groups consistently experience, there is a family feeling in the small-group experience such as we have at Community.

Family is really what Church is all about, apart from the current faddish focus on "family values." Long before that preferred phrase came into popularity and long after it has vaporized into the annals of popular culture, the Church will be focusing, as it always has, on the strengthening of individual families and the collection of families which constitutes a congregation or a movement or a denomination.

And what are the feeling tones of the Church family? Consider: The Church family is the place where untold uncles, and missing aunts, and forgotten grandfatherly figures, and seeming sisters and obvious brothers gather for story-telling, feasting, and a communion of spirits. The Church family is where old hurts are healed and new mistakes are forgiven. It is where there is always a place at the table for you, and where the fare is sprinkled with laughter and spiced with long-held hopes and dreams. The Church family is the home base where we get recharged and reconnected with our child-likeness and the potential for intimate warmth and committed caring within a safe and secure family-like setting. The Church family is sometimes "the only real family" some folks ever have these days, a noble substitution for the lack of caring and the absence of close contact brought about by our frenzied mobility. The Church family is sometimes even the last, best hope for someone about to give up on smiling, or sanity, or straightforward direction for their careers, or truth in their relationships.

Let us consider again the importance of our families in shaping our faith journeys, and the crucial importance of family integrity for the fuller fruition of the human community.

Dear Jack

(Community members and friends once inquired about my thoughts about news releases pertaining to the Vatican's statements (with then-Pope Benedict's full approval) about the Latin Mass, "The Church," and what they might mean for ecumenical dialogue. In response I composed the following piece, which is an "imagined letter" to a Catholic friend I call "Jack.")

Dear Jack–

After reading and rereading the news from the Vatican this week, it was good to speak with you over a cup of coffee at The Roasterie this morning. I'm grateful for the time and for your care and reassurances. A squall of consternation has darkened the skies of ecumenical dialogue in recent days, and the prospects for the kind of conversation that takes place among those who speak as equals has been dimmed. But I'm glad for your openness and am actually encouraged by what you described as your "disappointment" over the Vatican's recent actions and the Pope's endorsements of them. Your comments were not unlike those of John and Sue, Catholic friends in a parish different from yours with whom I shared lunch yesterday. Still I'm not yet persuaded by your assertions that most American Catholics are similarly disappointed (and perhaps embarrassed).

And thanks for the piece by Dr. Ann Riggs, Associate General Secretary for Faith and Order from the National Council of Churches. I have read with great interest her commentary about the Pope's release of "Responses to Some Questions Regarding Certain Aspects of the Doctrine on the Church."

But Riggs' statements, as well as clarifications from such open-minded Catholics as yourself and John and Sue, are not very reassuring. They would make more overall sense and feel more comforting if a person of some significant level of authority within the Roman Catholic Church itself would state outright: "Protestants are completely legitimate members of Christ's Body. Yes, we understand the folks in your churches to be Christians." To call us "ecclesial communities" is not really very

encouraging. And to refer to "defects" within the Orthodox
Church is hardly conciliatory. I recall Thom Savage, on
numerous occasions on our weekly Sunday morning radio talk-
show, *Religion on the Line*, stating that the Catholic Church
regarded Protestants as "fully Christian." That kind of
declaration was and remains truly reassuring for ecumenical
relations.

I should say again what you heard me say this morning:
Protestants neither need nor require statements such as Thom
Savage's to authenticate our faith. But such statements would
help to quell dismaying news reports and would serve as
springboards for greater ecumenical cooperation on some of the
world's truly pressing issues, like poverty and hunger.

It was interesting to imagine with you those audiences to
which the Pope might be sending indirect messages. To some,
I'm sure, both the reinvigoration of the Latin Mass and the
commentary about what and who constitute the "Church" are
like manna from heaven. For the followers of LeFebvre and
similar groups — those whom you long ago described as
"schismatics" and not in the mainstream of Roman Catholicism
— I'm sure this will hearten their hopes of a return to a pre-
Vatican II kind of Catholicism. If the documents were meant
mostly for internal restraining purposes, i.e., to rein in wayward
Roman Catholic theologians, then why release the documents
publicly?

For American Catholics, I can imagine a small minority
welcoming the Vatican's recent pronouncements. But a
significant portion of the American Catholic population may feel
even further alienated and distanced. I know some who are now
seeking out Protestant alternatives and are not in any way
intimidated from doing so. In fact, the Vatican's recent severity
in highlighting the differences among people in the Judeo-
Christian heritage may even spur on the departure of disaffected
Catholics. I also know countless Catholics who had thought their
branch of the Church had come a long way toward mending
relations with Jews, but are now wondering if a woefully
backward step has been taken.

I suppose the main sore point for Protestants could be this:
the statements coming out of the Vatican these days, which some
commentators say are really intended for Catholic audiences,
carry with them more than a hint of presumption. The

presumption? That any final assessment of faith matters — regarding the search for truth, authenticity, and closeness to God's heart of love — rests with papal authority. As you can imagine, such a presumption is overheard by many Protestants as insulting condescension.

On the other hand, on the other side of the aisle among mainline Protestants — who, as you well know, are the primary partners in ecumenical and interfaith conversations — there is a baseline and in some cases historic acceptance of Catholics as full-fledged members of the Body of Christ. You were exactly on target to remind me that there are certain fundamentalists and conservative evangelical Christians who will use these latest releases from Rome as fuel for their condemning bonfires of anti-Catholicism. And I believe I was right to remind us that they may hide such condemnation within the cozy caveat of "Oh, we don't condemn them, the Bible does."

Regarding the overall theological tug-of-war between Protestants and Catholics, I believe it's helpful (maybe even healing) to remember that John 3:16 says "God so loved the world that He gave His only Son," and not "God so loved the Church that He gave His only Son."

Regardless of the impact of Pope Benedict's comments within the Roman Catholic Church, Protestants, as we have for nearly 500 years, take our authenticating charge and authorizing mandate from a *magisterium* far larger, far grander, far more dynamic than any institutional expression of religion. Thus I will proceed with care and prayer to see how we at Community can do our part to stimulate better ecumenical dialogue and more compassionate service to a world much in need. Instead of driving us apart, this momentary contretemps just might be a stimulant for closer relations. Such is my hope.

Best Regards,

Bob Hill

Commencements

I've always treasured occasions of commencement. I've always cherished the joy shared by families at commencement, the sacred experience of saturating release once a worthy struggle is over, and the recognition of knowledge being passed on to new generations.

At commencement exercises there is a sense that miracles have occurred. And that is so because they have. The miracle of discovery. The miracle of rising after falling. The miracle of finishing after failing. The miracle of proficiency. The miracle of excellence. The miracles of transferring wonder and appreciation and intrigue and the glories of the universe — from mind to mind, from life to life.

Occasions of commencement are also simply splendid because of the word itself. Every commencement is a new beginning, a reminder that Yogi Berra was exactly right: "It ain't over til it's over."

Every commencement is an enrollment in a new moment in our maturation, moving us forward to the next phase of our development, and the next, and the next. Congratulations, graduates. May the commencements never cease!

Consecration

Consecration is not a word you spot every day in the newspaper or hear spoken very much on television or see very often on the internet. *Consecration* is probably not a word that comes readily to our tongues in the course of an average day. Yet, despite its rarity, it is one of the premier expressions for the dynamics of faith. You could say that consecration is a character accompanying every event and every aspect of meaningful activity in a congregation.

Consecration follows volunteers on their appointed weekly rounds, providing comfort here, advising daring there. Consecration serves as a playful connector as a happily expectant mother announces, "We're expecting!" Consecration cherishes the chance to hunker down in a nursery rocking chair and soothe a small one to sleep.

Consecration loves choir practice, singing each part with gusto. Consecration sits with compassion and supportive care at a funeral service, as family and friends grieve the death of a beloved one. Consecration thrives on study and reflection in Sunday School classes, weekly Bible study, and other special learning opportunities.

Consecration celebrates in all parent-child dedications, as loving parents present their newest gifts of life for blessing before the entire congregation. Consecration speaks up in prayers before meals and in benedictions at the end of committee meetings. Consecration nods its head in affirming love toward family members in a hospital waiting room, before, during, and after a surgery for a loved one. Consecration sits ready, leaning forward a bit in the chair, to offer help and aid in a pastor's study as sermons are prepared.

Consecration participates in outreach service projects, laughing, sharing, working, doing justice, transforming the world. Consecration cherishes the promises uttered at weddings and loves the butter mints at the receptions afterwards. Consecration hangs out wherever beauty abides, cannot tolerate cruelty, and always tries to make sure everybody has enough. Consecration loves to watch former adversaries become reconciled, lifts up a Hallelujah whenever a child of God escapes the strangulation of poverty, and sleeps soundly and best when peace accords are agreed upon and weapons are silenced.

Consecration never slouches in the presence of children or sloughs off anything or anyone as irrelevant or inconsequential. Consecration always takes seriously the lives of everyone and the witness of all faithful people. But Consecration is never overly serious and thus never tires of invitations to graduations, birthday parties, retirement galas, reunions, or any other occasion of celebration, whether quiet or rowdy.

Wherever you go this week, I hope and trust you'll experience Consecration as your constant companion.

Democracy

On Election Day, the marquee at Community Christian Church, 4601 Main Street, in the heart of Kansas City, Missouri, and in the heart of the heart of the country, broadcasts a simple statement: "Vote!" Americans once again will exercise the most toned musculature of any democratic republic in world history.

Not that we all exercise at the same pace or with the same intensity. And not that some folks still refuse to exercise at all. E.B. White, wry-witted *New Yorker* writer and beloved author of *Charlotte's Web,* was partially on target when he said, "Democracy is the recurrent suspicion that more than half of the people are right more than half of the time."

H.L. Mencken, as he was consistently wont to do, once offered a more cutting, cynical assessment of our political process: "Democracy is only a dream: it should be put in the same category as Arcadia, Santa Claus, and Heaven." I would quickly point out that such a comment is wrong on so many counts! And yet, Mencken was 100% half-right about democracy being a dream.

Before democracy is enacted and embodied in the shared congress and common commerce of a human community, it is indeed a dream.

Democracy is the dream of citizens ever striving to be more and more of what we say we are.

It is the dream of immigrants who have heard from afar about democracy's promise, have worked for it to become real in their lives, and have then tasted its full flavor when they actually have become citizens.

It is the dream of school children, as they learn of the sorely blemished but still blessed trajectory of the U.S. experiment with freedom over the past 232 years.

It is the dream of citizen groups, as their members organize and gather their collective will to press their cherished concerns.

It is the dream of all who want to live out the virtue of fairness.

Democracy is the dream of all who have been shackled politically, culturally, and physically by death-dealing totalitarian systems and deadly dictatorships.

It is the dream of everyone who reads the Declaration of Independence with deep discernment.

It is the dream of us all when we take seriously the gifts of diversity and the challenges of living in a pluralistic world.

It is the dream of each one who carefully interacts with the advance of new technologies and their impact on the global village.

It is the dream of every person who enters a voting booth mindful that theirs is not the final say but part of the main in our nation's grand laboratory of liberty.

F.O.R.G.I.V.E.N.E.S.S.

Over time I've grown less and less fond of acronyms for teaching and preaching purposes, but occasionally one will come upon me and seems worthwhile. Here's an acronym that some may find helpful regarding giving and receiving forgiveness:

F Face the humanity of the persons who have harmed you, recognizing that they, like you, are children of God.

O Overcome your need to enact revenge, to get back, to get even with the person who has wronged you.

R Release the person who has hurt you into the possibilities of a positive future; in other words, wish them well.

G Though we may not be able to forget, God does. What God forgives, God forgets.

I Internalize for yourself what you have externalized toward others. (Remember the wise advice of Anne Lamott: "It's futile to drink rat poison and then wait for the rat to die.") .

V Verify and validate your membership in the human community. (What is good enough for everybody else is good enough for you.)

E Embrace God's grace, exult in God's love, and make your exit. Go and sin no more!

N Never put a period where God has put a comma. (Thanks to Peter Gomes for this aphorism and whomever he borrowed it from.)

E Energize your prayer life each day with the saying of the Lord's Prayer, emphasizing the portion about asking for God's forgiveness as you forgive others.

S Sustain an attitude of forgiveness by breathing. Yes, breathing. In times of great duress and when a less-than-forgiving cloud swoops over the horizon of your life, simply breathe in and breathe out, relaxing your spirit.

S Start each new day with the realization that God has forgiven your broken yesterdays and has provided you bright new possibilities today.

Holy Spirit

There abides at the core of the Church's being a dynamic reality that empowers every Christian individually and all congregations collectively.

It is invisible to the naked eye, but so very manifest to the welcoming heart.

It attends every worship service on every worship day in every congregation on the face of the earth. But it cannot be contained within the confines of a church's walls.

It will participate in committee meetings, organizational gatherings, and planning sessions, if it is invited.

Sometimes it can be heard loud and clear, and sometimes it seems to be sleeping.

It is a divinely offered gift, democratically intended for all to take in and enjoy. Yet it is one of the most mysterious realities for Christians to understand or talk about. It is surely one of the most neglected elements of our foundational faith.

It's impossible to pin down, but you can pin all of your hopes on it.

It's as unpredictable as the weather, but it is as reliable as night turning into day.

It is different in kind and effect from its sibling sorts which enthuse the fans at Arrowhead on Sunday afternoons and the concertgoers at the Sprint Center or at Starlight Theater on a hot summer night.

It is an intercessor for us when we do not know how to pray, and a comforter in times of desperate need and quiet despair.

It reveals as it conceals; it demurely hints even when it overtly proclaims; it inspires great oratory and eloquence, and it can leave us speechless.

Where the Church is alive, it is there; wherever the Church has become debilitated, it has been made to feel unwelcome.

It burns warmly in the midst of the cold night on Christmas Eve; it flickers and flits and deepens the shadows throughout Lent; it gleams bright and fancy and full of holy power on Easter Sunday morning; and it shines like birthday cake candles when Pentecost comes.

It is the very essence of the air the Church breathes, and, in a tantalizing moment of wonder and awe-inspiring grace, it can take your breath way.

This dynamic reality, this power, this gift, this elusive yet ever-alluring essence is what we call "Holy Spirit."

Home

There are immense ranges of definitions of "Home," from the stolidly permanent to the fragile and transient. "Home is where the heart is," we say about that warm sense of place where we are always and ever comfortable and free. "Home is anywhere I hang my hat," we also say when we are experiencing more flux in our stations in life. And yet, there is usually an affirming connotation associated with "home" things, events, and happenings. Consider the wonders of "home"...

In baseball's always-beloved and yet currently-beleaguered structures, one's team regularly performs better during a "home stand," as we root and hope for our players to cross "home plate" with increased frequency as they magnify their "home-run" production.

Although we didn't really need a course in "home economics" to teach us so, we all intuitively know, especially the "homemakers" among us, that "home remedies" are certainly among the most effective for whatever ails us, and "homegrown" tomatoes are the juiciest.

News from the "home front" is always the most welcome, and "home health care" is a natural preference for many approaching their advanced years.

In our nostalgic remembrances of the ancient game of kick-the-can, there were always so-called discussions of which one of us reached "home base" first, and in business, the "home office" has more power, prestige, and permanence than the field sort.

"Homebuilders Associations" are proud of their endeavors to provide affordable new developments for proud new "homeowners," but none of us really, honestly lives in a "home on the range."

Couch-potato "homebodies" revel in that fact that television has even gotten into the act by proffering the wares of the movie industry via the "Home Box Office" channel, and we are all equally thrilled by the prospect of viewing old "home movies," or their newer cousins "home videos."

Whatever we do, we all look forward to "heading for home," knowing that the "home stretch" is always the most rewarding, aware that we, and all other "homeboys," will soon be "home free" in our "home sweet home."

There are also the wonders, comfort, and glory of "having a church home," an experience that is treasured by Community members and countless folks in umpteen congregations across the globe.

We are all of us searching for a sense of home, and for many now, and many more to come, that search finds fulfillment in being part of a vital congregation which helps us grow as persons.

Music is...

Music is a premier means of conveying inspiration, revelation, innovative ideas, and unparalleled emotions. When all other modes of communication fail, whether by circumstance, linguistic divergence, or lack of motivation, music can portray the heart's deepest desires, the mind's highest reach, and the soul's strongest longings.

In the religious realm, music is the language of God through which the eternal truths of the ages are relayed from one generation to another. Music, naturally, is central to our experience of faith in and through the Church. We are blessed at Community with wonderful music. Who doesn't prize the soaring solo, the energizing jazz-gospel chorus, the stirring movements of a choral masterpiece, the delicately rendered organ piece?

And how we cherish the singing of favorite hymns! In worship, we recall the telling truth of the quaint adage: "The one who sings prays twice." We agree with the researchers and sociologists who observe that newcomers and visitors, as well as current members of any church, rely upon good music for at least half of their experience of the holy in worship.

Music is also important at home, in our vehicles, at the workplace, even while we study. Music is the spice that gives life its fuller flavor. Music is soothing when everything else is rough. Music decorates the unseen interiors of our souls, just as paint and wallpaper decorate the visible walls of our homes.

Music inspires us individually; because of music we can breathe the air of the world with greater ease and purpose. Music also inspires us in a collective fashion; music is a necessary component of any virtuous community, a bond that helps us know and live with one another better.

Whether at a performance of the symphony, a blues festival, a choral recital, a rock concert, a classical opera, a coffee house, a jazz club, a folk jam session, or a chamber orchestra presentation, music serves to bind a city together. Music gives us a means by which the members of a diverse community can relate more cohesively.

Resurrection

No other facet of Christian faith challenges the cynic quite so quickly. No other tenet of Christian belief mystifies the skeptic quite so deeply. And no other feature of the Christian tradition continues to transform followers of Jesus so powerfully. Of course, I refer to the premier theme within the sanctions of Christian conviction: "Resurrection."

We call Sunday, April 24, "Easter," but we could just as easily call it "Resurrection Day." Wherever Easter is celebrated, it is done so with a focus on one of the most confounding and enthralling events in recorded human history: that Jesus was raised from death by God's powerful, loving grace.

We each have experienced crucifixions of one sort or another. In one person's life there is an unjust oversight for a promotion. In another person's life there is the struggle to overcome the undertow pull of drugs as one swims the seas of daily existence. In one family, there is the deep pang of loss and abandonment at the news of a loved one's accidental death. In another family, there is obvious torture experienced when news is shared about a cancer diagnosis. Yes, each of has experienced some sort of crucifixion at one time or another in our lives. In the midst of this fundamental reality, we can affirm the thesis and title of Rien Poortvliets amazing book of paintings which portray Jesus' life, ministry, crucifixion, and resurrection in anguished detail: *He Was One of Us.*

Jesus was indeed one of us. And, as we will enthusiastically proclaim in our opening processional Easter hymn at Community: "Made like him, like him we rise... ours the cross, the grave, the skies." Just as Jesus was one of us, we are his. And if the Easter hymn is right, then the resurrection is an absolutely indispensable, ultimately defining aspect of our identity and destiny as Christians.

So let us proclaim with joy and thanks those moments when the resurrection is made real again, in our own time, like in the time of Jesus' resurrection:

- whenever and wherever there is reconciliation between former enemies;
- whenever a war-torn village comes to know real peace,

and the families of that village, especially the children,
are provided consistent opportunities for growth and
flourishing;

- whenever a surgery patient receives a new lease on life;
- whenever a dyslexic student masters a reading or math
  assignment;
- whenever a family discovers a liberating way out of
  dreadful cycles of poverty and destitution and is
  liberated into the bright new frontier of security and
  sufficiency;
- whenever a child with low esteem finds his or her true,
  high value;
- whenever our elders are allowed to share their wisdom
  one more time;
- whenever ....

The recollection of resurrection could go on and on —
throughout eternity, we might even say!

Some New (Ironic) Takes on "Mercy"

"What is mercy?" The meanings of mercy have been plentiful and varied for a long time. Just recently I began wondering, in an ironic way, what some new takes on "mercy" might be, and came up with the following:

I am thankful to God for the "amnesia" of my family, who have consistently failed to remember how self-absorbed and obnoxiously confused one can be when one is 15.

I am thankful for the "rudeness" of my sister, who rudely awakened me to the fact that she needed a listening ear and comforting shoulder to cry on, and thus gave me an occasion to care for her.

I am thankful for the "loathing" of the communities of faith of which I have been a part, who have borne with complete faithfulness an unfailing loathing of all things that would hurt or hinder children and make them cry.

I am thankful for the "neglect" of my parents, who so consistently neglected to respond to those times — too numerous to count!! — when I did not live up to their dreams and hopes for me, but instead kept on dreaming and hoping on my behalf any way.

I am thankful for the "disregard" of my friends, who have disregarded and ignored those times when I have been less than my best self.

I am thankful for the "forgetfulness" of God, who has chosen to obliterate my mistakes, misgivings, and misdeeds, and who cannot recall — or so God says, in the Biblical witness and in countless revelations! — all of those actions in relation to which I have been carrying burdensome guilt. "Put it down," God says, "and forget it already. I have."

So, what is mercy? An undoing. An alpha-privative affirmation of the deathly denials of our experiences of need. These are the surface-scratchings on the immense stone of hopeful mercy that God bids us to stand upon, to rest upon, to stay alive upon, and thereby to be forgiven and free.

Such are the musings from this perch this week. Let us always be grateful for the unending mercies that are ours to cherish and share with one another. I would treasure a chance to see your own responses to the question about mercy.

Texts

I share with you some running ruminations about texts.
Texts are essentially conveyances of meaning. Texts are more
than books, but books are surely the first sort of texts we can
imagine, remember, or encounter as such. Between front cover
and back cover, between title page and "The End," sits the text --
of a fictional, page-turning, curiosity-burning potboiler novel, an
epic poem, a collection of essays, a gathering of photographs.
These are all texts, and we are all of us interpreting such things
millions of times a day, as we read books, newspapers,
magazines, newsletters, flyers, and more. At the very least, texts
are indeed conveyances of meaning through words.

But texts can really be more than words. There are
numberless oral and aural texts: radio shows, symphonic
performances, CD recordings, tapings of lectures, the lectures
themselves, instrumental-music solos, vocal-music solos, and
more. There is the oral text of a phone call in which the speaker
attempts to transfer a message of information, a question, or
relational chit-chat, and the listener, in turn, attempts not only to
hear attentively but also to listen with an ear toward a proper
interpretation of what the caller ultimately called about.

There are visual texts, as well. Many of them consist merely
of images or symbols, such as television commercials, billboards,
newspaper and magazine advertisements, and commercially
sponsored blimps.

There can even be, so the great cultural hermeneuts
(interpreters) of our day say, "sensory" (or tactile) texts: the
gathering of tingling emotions and rushing passions when a
wedding couple makes promises before God; the moment of
exhilaration when a hitter in a baseball game clobbers a fastball
with such power that it rockets out of the park; the instance of
tender forgiveness and holy healing between parent and child;
the touch and tug of caring among longtime friends; the sense of
sated satisfaction, experienced personally and communally, after
a sumptuously delicious meal. Yes, even feelings can be texts.

Which is to say, of course, that all things, all places and all
times are texts and, as such, impart meaning to our lives. The
task of those involved in faith communities, as always, is to

interpret, as best we can, the many wondrous meanings of all these texts, particularly the texts of the Bible, our experiences in prayers, and the overflowing amazement we experience in the presence of the God — who is "with us always." This is what our worship services are principally for; this is what preaching is all about, as well. The interpreting of texts remains a fascinating and thrilling task for me, and I hope it will continue to be so in your faith journey.

What Churches Are For

This week I'm giving thanks for the graces of Community's activity level this past month. It truly has been a great June! Just consider: our wonderful "Everywhere Fun Fair" Vacation Bible School; the exceedingly fine work of our Children's Ministry Council; the victorious energizing that was the MORE² banquet; the ongoing generosity of our Food Pantry, Micah Ministry involvements; and "Community Feeding the Homeless in the Park." Add to all of that the Kansas City Boys Choir concerts, the *Central Standard* extravaganza, and our Administrative Council's move toward the fulfillment of our capital campaign improvements in our sanctuary (new roof, new interior painting, and new carpeting), and we have more than we can ever say grace over. We can be appropriately excited about the possibilities for growth in all dimensions of our life together.

I believe there are certain ingredients which any congregation must possess if it desires to engage in the adventure of faith and the excitement of growth. And we have witnessed those ingredients at Community during the month of June.

Churches are always about **people**. Naturally, and to be sure, our worship is always expressed toward our Creator. And our teachings are about great and timeless sacred texts. And we exercise spiritual disciplines which focus our attention on the mysterious and the ineffable. But all of these endeavors are for naught if we forsake those whom the church is commissioned to help and heal: people.

Churches are sources of **power**. We are the carriers of a powerful message. We bear within our buildings and within our Christian witness the sign of the cross, one of the most powerful symbols the world has ever known. We are charged to proclaim the message of God's reconciling love with a spirit of power and not timidity. And who could deny the uplifting power of one of the Church's major traits, forgiveness? Equipping Christians with power is what the Holy Spirit is all about. The gift of power in people's lives is the Church's high calling.

Churches are empowered, first and foremost, by **prayer**. Prayer informs the maturing of our faith. Prayer motivates compassionate service toward others. Prayer grants release from guilt and quickens self-affirming resolve. Prayer connects us with our Creator and creates more possibilities for relationships with others. Prayer, humbly enacted and regularly practiced, in solo flight or in moving formation with others, can help us soar to the heights of spiritual understanding.

Of course, all churches have, and should have, a focus on their **properties**. But these are not properties in the physical sense, but rather in the more lasting, intangible sense. These are the characteristics and qualities which accent the Church's unique identity. And what are those Church properties which maintain the highest possible value? Properties such as commitment, sympathy, empathy, patience, kindness, justice, tenderness, joy, gladness, moral purposefulness, intelligence, hope, peace, and beauty. And what is that property which any Church must have lest its accounting sheet show a negative balance? It is that property which is called "a more excellent way," the property which is the essence of Christian faith and the God we worship, the property which makes us rich beyond measure and without which we are poor beyond description. The greatest property any Church can show on its ledger sheet is Love.

So, thanks Community, for being about people, power, prayer, and properties!

Work

How we work is at least as important as what we actually work at. In an age when the average American changes occupations and/or jobs 11 times during their working life, the attitude we bear through the changes is central to success and contentment. During this year's Labor Day holiday, let us consider carefully and prayerfully the ingredients for healthy and useful attitudes toward the work we do.

Let us remember first that working entails compensation in addition to a paycheck. Monetary wages do not necessarily attend meaningful and significant work.

I know older persons who work harder in their retirement years than they ever did during their workforce years. Their satisfaction is found in volunteering for good and great causes and thereby making a meaningful contribution to the wider community.

I know homemakers of all stripes — housewives and househusbands — who work mightily but don't receive a penny for their efforts. Their compensation is satisfaction in adding to the moral development of others, doing something they love doing, time with children and grandchildren, peace and fulfillment for their families, well-managed households, the happiness that a fulfilling partnership brings.

There are also students, from kindergarten to college, whose work is a daily and exciting challenge to them, though their compensation can hardly be calculated in the gross national product.

Simply put, without these forces for goodness in our society, our social fabric might very well come unraveled.

Let us also recall that our work, apart from the love of our families and our relationship with God, is our most valuable possession. Here I am adapting something I first heard James Carville describe when he was assessing his colorful career as a political consultant. Where he first learned such wisdom I do not know, but it rang true then and rings true now. Far away from raucous political campaigns and the calumny of adversarial relationships with the media, Mr. Carville mused eloquently about work — any persons work — and its significance on the earthly scales of what counts as important.

My questions each Labor Day remain: Do you regard your work in such a manner? Do our communities regard our work in such a manner? Does U.S. culture? Is work one of your more prized possessions? How might your work become even more so?

Let us also remember that good work, well done, fit for a good purpose, shaped for the sharing of the wider community, is always a cherishable treasure. When we do such work, we are then engaging in what Marge Piercy describes so beautifully as "being of use."

HIGH HOLY DAYS

All the Saints!

At Community, the first Sunday of November is observed as All Saints Sunday, when we pay tribute to the faithful witnesses who have gone before us, particularly those of our members who have died in the previous 12 months and whose memory we treasure.

On this day we note once more the themes of transience, mortality, and change which touch every human life. In this moment of celebration, we learn again that:

(1) our faith is an inheritance;

(2) we abide in a long line of rich traditions;

(3) there are more possibilities within God's hopes for us than there are setbacks and shortcomings in us; and

(4) the treasuring of the past empowers the present and future expressions of the church's ministries and bears witness to Christ's ways in the world.

As we anticipate this year's All Saints Sunday, I'm mindful of the words of the apostle Paul, who reminds us of the utterance which all of us would cherish as a benediction after our journeys have come to fulfillment: "I have fought a good fight, I have finished my course, I have kept the faith."

Let's also remember Oscar Wilde's encouragement: "Every saint has a past, and every sinner has a future."

And I would say that Soren Kierkegaard was absolutely on the mark when he observed: "God creates out of nothing. Wonderful, you say. Yes, to be sure, but he does what is still more wonderful: he makes saints out of sinners."

Thankful for Thanksgiving

This year, amidst the myriad blessings that shower down on us all, I'm more thankful than ever for the American Thanksgiving holiday itself.

Thanksgiving is surely our most inclusive celebration as a nation, honoring all people and their ties to one another, from every station and every status, every race and every place, sometimes brought about by duress and crisis, just as the original Thanksgiving celebrants knew all too well.

Thanksgiving is the most straightforward of our holidays: a door is opened into a welcoming home (or a restaurant), a table is spread, food and laughter (and occasionally a few tears) are shared, words of gratitude to God grace the day. Simple. Straightforward.

Thanksgiving is the most community-minded holiday we know, since we sometimes welcome as many friends as we do family members to our tables on Thanksgiving Day.

Thanksgiving is also the least commercial of our holidays, requiring no gift exchanges or extravagant purchases in response to enticing ad campaigns.

Thanksgiving just may be the most "friend-producing" holiday for Americans. Recall how acquaintances who met for the first time at a Thanksgiving gathering have become dear friends over the years.

And Thanksgiving is the most eclectic culinary holiday we know as Americans, with families sharing their delectable fares with gusto, gastronomic pleasure, and amazing variety.

For these and many other reasons, I will offer special words of thanks for the Thanksgiving holiday itself this year.

Giving Thanks for Common Things

Thanksgiving is one of my favorite holidays, and the whole month of November seems to me like one of the most delightful seasons one could ever imagine.

As we enter deeply into Thanksgiving celebrations, I'm taking a moment (a bunch of moments, in fact) to give thanks to God for the common things, the daily graces, that are ours when we're...

eating dinner
or
washing the dishes
or
taking a walk
or
doing the laundry
or
paying the bills
or
talking to a friend on the phone
or
mowing the lawn
or
raking the leaves
or
pruning a tree
or
reading the Bible
or
taking out the trash
or
bringing in the mail
or
leaving for work
or
listening to thunder
or
filling a glass with water
or

pouring a cup of coffee
or
gazing at a candle
or
coming home from work
or
changing a diaper
or
driving through the neighborhood
or
laughing at a silly joke
or
slicing an apple
or
perusing a book
or
watching a DVD
or
going to the movies
or
enjoying a concert
or
tasting a birthday cake
or
reading a letter
or
writing a note
or
sending an email
or
musing on the light caressing the face of the earth at sunset.

In all of these moments let there be within us a welling-up of profound thanks for the blessed privilege of life, for the extraordinary grace of existence, and for God being with us each step of the way.

Advent and Christmas

Advent and Christmas comprise a period in the church calendar that can be described as a season of gifts. Truly there is no better time for faith enrichment in the church, as time-honored and sustaining truths recapture our attention, as new insights and new reflections rejuvenate our faith, as beautiful colors and dazzling lights enchant our eyes, as favorite carols quicken our dreams, and as actual material presents are given to show forth our love of God and love of one another.

This year during Advent and Christmas, I hope and trust that you will experience anew the priceless gifts of this season. Be sure to make room under your tree, around your hearth, and within your heart for the following:

The Gift of Time — Frazzled by the hectic pace of it all? Burdened by the shopping lists and personal registry of responsibilities? Offended by the visage of one more television holiday commercial? Then take some time out to rest, reflect, ponder the true worth of this holy season. Renew your religious convictions with a quiet prayer each day. Revitalize your most important relationships with family and friends alike with some gentle time of togetherness.

The Gift of Worship — The four Sundays of Advent leading up to Christmas, the arrival of the Christ Child celebrated on Christmas Eve, and the special worship services arrayed throughout this season are rare and fine gifts. Ask folks what some of their favorite worship services are, and they'll quickly recall the services they experienced during this sacred season in the past. For so many, this is a time of extraordinary broadening and deepening of religious convictions. And, please note: as you give yourself and your family and friends the exquisite graces of worship and disciplined devotion, you'll receive so many other additional gifts as well.

The Gift of Music — Music is an overflowing benefaction during this holy time of year. There is no more inspirational music than the music that is sung, played and heard throughout Advent and Christmas. Even music selections (such as sections of Handel's *Messiah*) which ordinarily should be set within our Easter celebrations gravitate toward Christmas. The music of this season inspires our souls, soothes our minds, encourages our hearts, and binds our lives together in a harmony of hope.

Christmas Music

The continuous streams of great music which course over, around, and through our Advent and Christmas celebrations are simply amazing. At this time of year, we are reminded that there really is hope for the fruitful living of our days and the sharing of our faith journeys together. Nothing can communicate that holy resilience better than the music of this season.

And behold the wondrous diversity of the music! Witness: "A Chipmunk Christmas," Elvis' "Blue Christmas," the "Appalachian Dulcimer Christmas," Dolly Parton's "Hard Candy Christmas," the Mormon Tabernacle Choir's version of Handel's *Messiah*, Tchaikovsky's *Nutcracker*, Jessye Norman's version of "Sweet Little Jesus Boy," Tim Whitmer's "Plaza Tidings," Nat King Cole's "The Christmas Song," the Beach Boys' "Christmas Luau," the Harlem Boys Choir's "Little Drummer Boy," Bing Crosby's "White Christmas," John Fahey's haunting guitar in his *Christmas Album*, or Charlie Brown's *Charlie Brown Christmas*. And witness, as well, all the extraordinary musicians — in every club and jazz-happening place — who grace us with their stellar talents in Kansas City during the Christmas season! And....The list could go on and on!

As always, we are blessed to behold the energizing power of beautiful music that is part of Community's special presentations during this time of year, and in all other congregations that take seriously the call to "make a joyful noise unto the Lord." There really are no better "music events" at Community, or elsewhere, than during this season's many occasions of singers, musicians and congregation raising irrepressibly deep and joyful sounds of praise and celebration.

I hope and trust that you will allow the great music of this season to touch your life and give you fresh inspiration and glad joy. There is always cause for excitement as we honor Christ's presence in our midst. But there are compounded reasons for elation at this time of year, when we renew our awareness of that presence and double our celebrations.

So, join in the singing, add another carol to your "favorites" list, affirm those who are making special presentations of beautiful music (at Community and elsewhere), appreciate the unique ways by which music can communicate the deepest of human longings and the highest gifts from the divine, and, as always, "make a joyful noise unto the Lord."

Some Items for a Christmas Gift List

Some items for a Christmas gift list:

To give:
words of affirmation for those you love the dearest;
prayers for those you don't know at all;
food for those who are hungry;
donations for shelter and medical supplies for those in disaster
situations;
a bit of beauty to those who may have previously known only
ugliness;
songs of joy in any and all despairing circumstances.

To receive:
hope in the face of crisis;
courage in the presence of danger;
humility in the wake of pride;
joy to make all days bright;
love to counter all indifference.

To give and receive:
sharing that is full of shalom;
fellowship that is full of faith;
insights gained from scripture;
hearts ever growing in the hope for peace.

Lent: A Many Splendored Season

For some seekers of the sacred, the season of Lent is a holy disruption. The span of time between the arrival of Ash Wednesday and the ensuing 40 days leading up to Easter Sunday (minus, of course, the Sundays during the season which are regarded as "little Easters") is a time of orientation, disorientation and reorientation. Since Christmas we've been moving through time in a fairly smooth manner. Then comes an instant when we're a bit befuddled and bedazzled, caught in a surreal disturbance of the normal. This happens for the seasoned Christian as well as for the novice, for elders as well as for the young, for adults as well as for children.

Some have described it as being an unwitting character in a snowglobe that's suddenly shaken up. For other folks it's like that moment in a movie theater when, after settling into your seat with popcorn and candy, after the endless previews, it's time for the main event. All of a sudden, for the life of you, you can't recall the title of the movie you're about to see. In that instant of virtual vertigo, you're existentially adrift. But then you do recall, and you shift your attention into gear, and the space and time of your world make sense.

For other seekers and sojourners Lent is a continuing pageant of great power. Lessons learned in Sunday School about humility and hope are held in symbolic relief as a family comes forward during an Ash Wednesday service to receive "the imposition of ashes." At Community a Palm Sunday parade through the Plaza will inspire participants and onlookers alike. This year's revival of the dramatic "The Living Last Supper" will impress worshipers with the wondrous mix of divinity and humanity in Jesus presiding over the last meal he would share with his first followers. Majesty. Heightened humility. Dramatic portrayals. Theater of the ultimately real. An ongoing pageant of great power.

Whether disruption or pageantry, Lent helps to shape and transform our faith. May the shapings and the transformations lead each of us to a closer walk with God, greater love toward all neighbors, and personal fulfillment unlike any we've known before.

Lent's ABCs

The Lenten season is really very simple and straightforward, as uncomplicated and elementary as our ABC's. Consider...

I. ASHES Lent is, of course, all about ashes. That's how the journey begins, with ashes of repentance and humility on the forehead. The ashes remind us of the dustheaps of life which too many have known for too long. The ashes also remind us of the hollowness of our material possessions and how solid are the authentic and lasting verities of faith. A dusty smudge on one's forehead rekindles in us an awareness that human life is as fragile as ashes hovering in midair, drifting and fleeting in the wind. The ashes remind us to be careful and to be kind and to be ever gentle.

II. BLOOMING Lent is a time for focusing on blooms and the event of blooming. Far from being a time to be driven down into the depths of guilt and shame — a stereotype about the Lenten season to which we should say good riddance, once and for all!! Lent is a time for the nurturing and nourishment of the capacity for blooming within the human personality.

A new talent discovered. A new skill shared with another in need. A gift given for the betterment of the community. A new word of healing forgiveness. A cup of cold water. An instance of comfort...

All these are seeds of God's love which eventually bloom throughout a world in need. It is seasonally appropriate and historically understandable that Lent's culmination at Easter should parallel nature's verdant blooming in springtime.

III. COMPASSION And Lent is always an interval for proclaiming and reclaiming God's compassion for a world bruised, broken, and in need of restoration.

Recall Jesus' "Sermon on the Mount." Compassion. Recall Jesus' parable concerning The Prodigal Son and the Loving Father and his parable about The Good Samaritan. Compassion. Recall Jesus' searing invitation to his disciples that "when you did to one of the least of these, my brethren, you did it to me."

Compassion. Recall one of Jesus' most haunting pronouncements from the cross: "Father, forgive them, for they know what they do." Again, compassion.

If Lent's meaning could be thematically distilled into one substance, it would be the clear, sparkling, unadulterated essence of God's compassion for a hurting humanity.

Let us learn our Lenten ABC's anew this year with a fresh and sure purpose.

L.E.N.T.

Love is at the heart of Lent. As the days lengthen, as the season of spring approaches and anticipation mounts for the arrival of Easter's surprising gift, there is a heightened awareness of love and all of its implications for our lives. Love is the reason for human life itself. Love is the basis for our getting up in the morning. Love is the foundation for all of our efforts as people of faith. Love is the cornerstone of any strong home. Love is the source of support and affirmation we need to endure the rough portions of the paths we travel. Love is the giver of peace at day's end. Love bears through all hurt-filled experiences. Love believes in God's goodness in all daunting circumstances. Love hopes in all desperate situations. Love endures all seemingly unendurable losses.

Embracing is what Lent is to be used for. Embracing practices and disciplines of prayer. Embracing new angles of understanding on traditional themes and symbols. Embracing a community of faith and allowing oneself to be embraced by that same community. Embracing our families with a keener sense of God's presence in our midst. Embracing the world in all of its awe-full beauties and audacious wonders. Lent is definitely, as the book of Ecclesiastes would put it, a time for embracing.

Newness is also what Lent is all about. Lent also has to do with vitality for the new. Taking on a new task, a new way of Bible study, a new posture toward that which we call spiritual, a new risk in the faith's great ventures, a new perspective on a new subject of inquiry, a new small group experience, a new grasp of Jesus' teachings and saving ways, a new friend, a new group of friends, a new attitude in our relationships with God. Lent is that time when we remember the grand promise of God to make all things new.

Time that is extraordinary is Lenten time. Time and eternity intersect in the carpenter rabbi Jesus of Nazareth, and the world is never the same thereafter. Lent is a time for reflecting upon our hectic schedules and our crammed agendas and having too much stuff to do. Lent is the special moment when we discover that our time is not really ours at all but rather it is God's time. We may even discover, for the first time ever, what the Psalmist knew three millennia ago, that God has been our dwelling place in all generations... from everlasting to everlasting... and, thus, it is good for us to count our days that we may gain a wise heart.

8 Great Days of Holy Week

The eight days between the pomp and passion of Palm Sunday and the joyful resurrection of Easter Sunday comprise eight extraordinary "punctuation marks" in the drama of the Christian journey of faith. As we approach this year's Holy Week commemoration, consider the following observations.

Palm Sunday — With pageantry and palms we dramatize again the triumphant entry of the carpenter from Nazareth into the bustling city of Jerusalem. But the pomp and exultation will not last. Let this be a day for true and festive jubilation, and let us be keenly aware of the fickle character of popularity and acclaim.

Mundane and Magnificent Monday — While the adjectives used to describe this particular day have not been codified on any religious calendar, they do depict what most of our Mondays are like, a mixture of the mundane and the magnificent. Consider the possibilities which this particular Monday poses for you. Where will you encounter traces of the magnificent? Will they be found within the common? Will they be experienced within our routine, day-to-day actions?

Tuesday, A Day for Truth — Of course, every day is a day for truth. But it won't harm us to heighten our awareness of our crucial need for abiding in the truth. Consider how Jesus gave us his sterling example, not only of telling the truth, but also in being the truth. Recall Pilate's interrogating question "What is truth?" and then remember Jesus' response: he stands there and lets his life speak for him.

Musical Wednesday — Not only is Wednesday the occasion for our Chancel Choir's and our Journey Band's rehearsal sessions, but it's also a time for recollecting the great music that has congregated around the events of Holy Week and especially Easter. Nearly every great classical composer has created a masterpiece or two around the events of Holy Week. Next to Christmas, this week is undoubtedly the time for the best musical inspiration. Let us all listen for the Word proclaimed in wonderfully euphonic sounds — in worship, in various media, in our homes, and in the hallways of our memories.

Maundy Thursday — This day is set as a day for recalling the new love commandment (*maundate*, in Latin) which Jesus gave his disciples. Jesus' love for his disciples and the world was exquisitely manifested in the Lord's Supper. Thereafter the disciples' loving response to Jesus was and is renewed in acts of loving kindness, courage, and bold joy, day by day, but especially on this specific Thursday.

Good Friday — Even though the clouds roll in front of the sun, and the crucifixion occurs in all of its harsh brutality, and the disciples "all fall away," and death and destruction seem to prevail all too frequently in too many lives, still we call this day "Good Friday." Why? Perhaps because, while things may be bad, the worst has been overcome. Perhaps because, in some mysterious way, the ultimately good purposes of God are coming to fruition. Perhaps because the only way out or around is through.

Holy Saturday — A respite of sorts, a day for waiting, a time for deep reflection and a reassessment of our hopes and dreams, this Saturday poses a "between-the-times" kind of opportunity. We are in a vigil between the death of Jesus and the resurrection of the risen Christ, between the expectations of our earthly desires and the fulfilling provisions from God's generous heart, between then and now, between death-after-life and life-after-death. Let us wait and watch and allow our souls to wonder.

Easter Sunday — Easter is one loud, long, beautiful blast of proclamation, barely in need of embellishment. Let the word go forth: Christ is risen! Christ is risen indeed! On this eighth day, we behold creation anew. Resurrection is a reality not only for Jesus Christ back then and there, but also for all of God's children here and now. Celebrate this great good news!

Holy Week Blessings Are Coming

Holy Week is weighted — by tradition, experience, and imagination — with tremendous meanings and life-transforming consequences. Just as Christ's life is a fulcrum in the midst of human history, so the remembrances and liturgies of Holy Week serve as decisive turning points on the Church's calendar and in the hearts of Jesus' followers.

This year's Holy Week events at Community offer ample occasions and opportunities for grand spiritual deepenings. Consider the following guide for your journey through Holy Week and be wonderfully blessed.

Palm Sunday The launching of a week of palms and passion, triumph and trial. Rejoice with Christ's entry into Jerusalem and remember his generous mercy for the world.

Meditative Monday A day to consider the greatness of Christ's loving compassion. Prayerfully meditate on the places where Christ is being made known to people in need.

Tender Tuesday A day to affirm that tenderness is needed everywhere. Decide to make a gift of time, treasure, or talent to anyone or any place within your realm of influence where bruising or brutality has been experienced.

Wondering Wednesday A tipping-point time, full of quiet reflection and mixed anxious wondering. Engage in learning at noontime about love, and embrace the gifts of healing and wholeness in the evening.

Maundy Thursday An evening of recollection of Christ's shadowed trek toward an ultimate confrontation with the world's principalities and powers. A moment for sharing bread and cup and prayer.

Good Friday A day of mute awe and reverence, retracing the griefs of the early disciples and the world's indifference, and contemplating Christ's "Seven Last Words from The Cross."

Sacred Saturday An interlude for waiting and anticipation, an in-between time of uncertainty and restless hoping.

Easter Sunday The Resurrection Day full of joy and jubilation, affirmation and acclaim, feasting and festivities, celebrations through and through and all around!!

EASTER - *Remembrance, Reality, Resonance, Ray of Hope*

Easter arrives this Sunday, and we will celebrate it to the hilt. I believe the following are among the multitude of profound meanings of Easter.

Easter is a remembrance. At Eastertime, our hearts quicken when we hear the stories of Jesus' resurrection, recorded in each gospel and given testimonial affirmation in the accounts of the early Church's development.

It is a sacramental act to recall the first resurrection. It is not insignificant that one of Jesus' greatest bequests to his original band of disciples was his institution of the Lord's Supper in which he charged them (and us), "Do this in remembrance of me." According to Luke's gospel account, it was the startling remembrance of that last supper that awakened in Jesus' grieving followers the amazing good news of his triumphant resurrection.

Easter is a reality. We remember the resurrection of Christ and not merely the resuscitation of a body. Resurrection is the real transformation of a life and thereby Life itself and human history thereafter.

Zealous fact-finders and disbelieving skeptics may try to disprove the occurrence of the resurrection. But the resurrection is not a matter of indisputable factoids but of faith. Want to encounter a resurrection? Witness a reconciliation, or hold a newborn baby, or take the pulse of your soul, or behold the underlying mantle of mercy in the eventual resolution of human affairs.

Easter is not a matter of testing but of testimony. When we ponder Christ's resurrection as it is given testimony in the lives and love of Christ's followers, we see: Something really happened!

Easter is a resonance. Christ's resurrection was not the only statement God was making at the first Easter. Easter is about real life in real time, about our lives in our time.

On this side of the first resurrection, we hear the words of the earthly Jesus with fresh sensitivity: "I have come that you may have life and have it abundantly." As the apostle Paul knew down to the marrow of his bones, "He who raised the Lord Jesus will raise us also."

In our sacramental recollections we understand that something timeless and eternal interrupted the normal course of life and made us what we are today and will make us into new creations tomorrow and forever. God's resurrecting love echoes in our own hearts, and we are bid to listen and believe.

Easter is a ray of hope. Easter arrives in all of its glory when we are humble and open enough to hope. Undeterred despairing in the face of the dawn, adopting cynicism as a life posture, committing sarcasm in the midst of community — each is an arrogant presumption.

Because of Christ's resurrection and the promise of our own, we know some new truths: There is always more mercy in God than there is meanness in us. There is always more forgiveness in God than there are failings in us. And there is always more life in God than there is death in us.

Because Easter is a ray of hope, no one need ever give up in the struggles of life. Because Easter is a ray of hope, we can not only go on and endure; we shall, with God's resurrecting grace, prevail.

I'm looking forward to this year's Easter celebrations more than I have in years! May Easter be the most powerful and profound renewal of your faith you have ever known.

Easter Is...

We will soon arrive at the high-water mark of our Christian heritage, Easter, the most festive Lord's Day of the entire year.

Easter is the pulse at the heart of Christian faith. It is the ultimate motivation for weekly worship. It is the prime cause behind daily devotion. It is the launching pad for regular service and steadfast study.

Easter is a sacred surplus, inspiring us to shout with joy, "My cup runneth over..." It is a holy hilarity, causing us to laugh with delirious love. It is an unconquerable bond, safeguarding all of our hopes and worthy dreams.

Easter is the undercurrent in all the New Testament gospel accounts of Jesus' life and ministry, from beginning to end, subtle and overt, in all moments high and low. In precept, parable, and prayer, Easter's theme of new life suffuses all that Jesus says and does.

Easter is the foundation of all Christian theology. It is the reason for any and all ecclesial seasons observed by followers of Jesus of Nazareth. It is the sine qua non for each and every Christian celebration.

Easter is the undergirding for all of the Church's mighty music proclaiming God's triumphant grace. It is the stimulus for the loftiest poetry and the boldest declarations associated with Joseph's carpenter son turned wonderworking rabbi.

Easter is an event and a series of events. It is an array of actions. Easter is as much a verb as it is a noun. It is this active quality of the most special day on the church's calendar that inspired Gerard Manley Hopkins to coin the phrase "Eastering."

Easter is what makes possibility possible. It is what makes generosity generous. It is what makes new life new.

Easter is without a doubt the grandest occasion for celebrating which Christians can experience. For this reason you have heard Community's clergy emphasize the opportunities we all have to invite others to worship during this time of year, and especially for Easter Sunday worship.

Easter is an experience and an event and an array of actions for which countless souls seek confirmation, year by year, season by season, century by century. One theologian famously described how most people come to church on a Sunday, and particularly on Easter Sunday, to hear a response to a perennial question: "Is it still true?" This Easter Sunday we will proclaim loud and clear, "Yes, it is still true! Christ is risen! Christ is risen indeed!"

Easter Is Upon Us

Easter is upon us and not a moment too soon. The world needs Easter. Christians honor Easter as a crucial essential in a multitude of ways. For it is in the declaration of God's powerful love triumphing over all obstacles through Christ's resurrection that we truly know the ultimacy of God's grace.

What will Easter be like for you this year? What is Easter's salient meaning for you, as you contemplate its significance for the living of your days? Consider the following...

Easter is the outbreak of peace in the middle of a war-torn country. It is a festival and an annual remembrance and a treasured holiday, all for the sake of declaring "Love conquers all!" It is the springtime rising to sunlight of newborn blooms planted in the fall. And it is more.

Easter is a whispered word of encouragement in the midst of tragedy. It is a shout of acclamation in the thrall of unfettered joy. It is the yearly, measured, constant beating of God's drum of devotion for every man, woman and child on the face of the earth. And it is more.

Easter is the assumption that a divine Love woos and wins all human hearts through the unfearing truth of Christ's gentleness. It is the arrival of rain after a long drought and the rising of the sun after a deluge. Easter is obviously in the rain. And it is obviously in the sun. And it is irrefutably in the rainbow. And it is more.

Easter is a touch that heals the brokenhearted and a truth that makes tender the hardhearted. It is the astonishing good news that the past is only prelude, and that there is always more graciousness in God than there is reckless sin in us. It is the reassuring announcement that God's largesse ultimately prevails in the human saga. And it is more.

Easter is always more than we can ever imagine or fathom, and yet it is a gift we welcome with open arms and hearts.

Easter rises with determination in the face of ugliness and delights with ecstasy in the face of beauty. It inspires the disenchanted and the dispirited, and it humbles the brazen and the haughty. It causes all boats to rise with the lifting tide of human compassion.

Easter surprises all disillusioned ones who despair of any progress and comforts all wide-eyed dreamers who trust that the will of a caring Creator will come true.

Easter echoes through the canyons of human affairs with an undying affirmation from Gods eternal heart of mercy: "No matter what you do in all of your unseemly foolishness, I will not be kept from caring for each and every one of you, each and every day of your lives. I sent Christ, the Loving One, to show that my promise is true and to make it available for all of you forever!"

Easter Is Here

With the celebration of Easter we have arrived finally —
exultantly, gladly, happily, joyously — at the culmination of the
entire impetus of the Christian calendar. It is true, on the one
hand, that without Christmas there would have been no Easter.
But it is equally true, on the other hand, that without Easter
there would be no reason for celebrating Christmas.

So we are here! The time for pulling out the stops and letting
out the sails and cranking up the volume has come.

Such a festive approach to Easter is so naturally good, and I,
for one, can easily get taken up in all the hoopla. That's what
Easter seems to be all about: one long loud blast of proclamation.
Yet there are other views and angles on this most celebratory of
days on the Christian calendar, and those different perspectives
are to be honored as well.

Consider the reaction of fear and trepidation, such as the
gospel of Mark contains at its conclusion. There was no little fear
in the faces of those who beheld the evidence of the first
resurrection. Christ's resurrection, or any other sort of
resurrection for that matter, can be described with wary
adjectives: unusual, strange, ripe with the sorts of sights and
sounds — or lack of them — that upsetting trepidations are
made of. If one of our dearest departed friends suddenly arose
from death, we'd be full of fear and trepidation, too, I suspect.

And then, remember, there was the wonder and the
confusion, as the gospels of Luke and Matthew depict the mood
and manner of the apostles after they had heard of the rising of
their teacher and master Jesus. No wonder they wondered!
Doesn't Jesus' resurrection (not just a resuscitation) promote
some great theological problems — in addition to the scientific,
logical consequences it poses — for any level-headed, regular
human being? No wonder we have kept on wondering!
Wondering and standing misty-eyed in the face of God's
mysterious love, which possesses a power great enough to hush
the shout of death — perhaps that is all one can muster in
response to Easter.

And let us not forget the release from bondage, the release
from our bondages which Easter offers — out of anxiety, out of

hatred, out of self-loathing, out of a cosmic case of the dumps, out of division, out of separation itself, out of hopelessness, out of the grave -- and into freedom -- into love, into caring for others and others caring for you, into a clear horizon free of shadowy shame, into a future refreshed by a rain of joy, into forgiveness, into life, into life eternal.

Whether we focus on its unbridled exultation, fearful trepidation, wondrous confusion, or loving release, Easter is here for you and you and you and you, and for me, for all of us. It is here for us to embrace. One thing is for certain: no matter how we take it, Easter is God's declaration of eternal love for all creation, and God will not be thwarted in having the last word. Let's greet each other this coming Easter Sunday with deep appreciation for God's great declaration and then let us respond with a declaration of our own: "Christ is risen! Christ is risen indeed!"

Pentecost Is the Church's Way of Celebrating Its Birthday

Pentecost is the Church's way of celebrating its birthday.

The color for Pentecost is festive and fiery red, reminding us of the "tongues of fire" which seemed to rest above and on the heads of the believers who gathered in Jerusalem 50 days after the resurrection and who were overwhelmed by a wonderful Spirit of empowerment.

The themes for Pentecost are remembrance and hope, or, in other words, rekindling our appreciation of all that has transpired before us and inclining us toward an ultimately proper direction — the future — for any congregation worthy of thriving.

The purpose of the entire event is, of course, glad celebration. We commemorate the Church's birthday with glad rejoicing because it is finally a celebration which gives us a sense of understanding and incorporation of an event into the very fabric of our lives.

Celebration is one of the key components for optimum functioning in our personal, family, social lives.

Celebration is the explicit recognition of thriving in the world.

Celebration is to life as punctuation is to writing. Periods, question marks, and exclamation points finalize so that we can grasp a whole thought or concept. Without punctuation it would be extremely difficult to make meaning of what we are reading. Without celebration, it is extremely difficult to incorporate the meanings of experience and life itself.

By celebrating the Church's birthday, we recognize the thriving of Christ's followers in the world and are better able to incorporate the meaning of faith in our lives. We also celebrate the Church's birthday because birthday parties are simply fun, fundamentally enjoyable, and good for the human community.

Let us celebrate with glad hearts this coming Sunday, as we observe the 1978th birthday (give or take a few years) of the Church.

PRAYER

In Praise of Prayer

Prayer is the soul's cry. It is conversation and communion with the Holy One. Prayer is, at once, the deepest need and the highest hope of humanity. It is the place and the time and the mood in which God meets us.

All prayers, even our bumbling ones, can be transformed into true union with God. All prayers, even our struggling, hesitant, ignorant, hobbled ones, are received by God.

In prayer we enter into an intentional yearning for a holy touch, a holy word, a holy sign of reassurance. Sometimes our yearning is borne along wordlessly, a simple ache from the deepest interior part of us. At other times, our yearnings achieve symphonic status, echoing beauty and grandeur.

There is no place and no situation in which prayer — either as a primary or an accompanying yearning — is not appropriate. There is no person or group from whom prayers cannot emanate.

Prayer is as old as the human saga and as new as sunrise. Prayer — humble, reaching, compassionate, honest, transparent prayer — stands at the core of any faith worth having.

Prayer is not superstition but that which liberates us from the muck of superstition. Prayer is not the veneration of any material object or geographical location but that which conveys sanctity and honors objects and places which, thereafter, we call holy.

Prayer can be enacted standing up, sitting down, lying prone, awake or asleep. Public prayers can be and have been some of the most inspirational instances of glorious rhetoric ever witnessed by human beings. And yet the most lyrical, lovely, and altogether beautiful prayers anyone can ever know are those offered in simple solitude.

Prayer at the Center

At the center of our religious journey is the experience of prayer — in solitude, in public, aloud, silently, with the use of a prepared text, spontaneously in the inspiration of the moment. Prayer is at once the most valuable among our connections with God and an ever-elusive discipline which defies any final categorization. Ask a hundred people their understanding of prayer, and they will offer a hundred different descriptions. Yet we do no harm and a world of good by investigating again and again this elusive essential in our lives. Consider the following meanings of prayer:

Prayer is a dialogue with one's Creator, in one's own time and place, using the unique lexicon of love. Prayer sometimes seems like a monologue, with only a faint hint of a whisper of response from the divine; but then, later, a response comes, when we least expect it, and the response is full of promise and hope and fulfillment.

Prayer is meant for thanksgiving. When a baby is born, when a child takes the first step, when release from oppression is obtained, when pain ceases, when disease is overcome, when reconciliation is consummated, when the harvest is brought in, when milestones are achieved, when the novel is finished, when the promotion announcement is heard — all these inspire the simple words "Thank You," and, more often than we ever realize, it is God's hand which has wrought such inspiring, thankful moments.

Prayer is also meant for cleansing our lives, almost as if our lives were houses. Consider how "the house of your life" has sometimes contained... closets of confusion, nooks and crannies of confoundedness, a living room made dingy by loneliness, a den of defensiveness, a porch of perplexity. Prayer helps us "clean house."

Prayer is, of course, certainly an act of petitioning — not as we do for political candidates in the momentary occasion of a campaign, but steadily, day by day, on behalf of those we love and on one's own behalf. When life is stretched to its extremities, when we seem to be hanging onto hope by the slenderest of threads, we typically ask for help. It is almost unnatural not to do so. And there is absolutely nothing inappropriate to bring before God. (We may not receive the answer we had wanted but we always receive the answer we ultimately need.) The saints and sages of the ages continuously impressed their belief in this truth, that God always prefers engagement to disregard, that painful expressions of ire and dissatisfaction are always more pertinent than is the silence of indifference.

So let us be about the business of the humbling, ennobling, energizing, quieting, enlivening and calming experiences of prayer.

Prayers We Love to Pray

I hope and trust you have some favorite prayers. I hope and trust you'll find some that you can hang your heart on, prayers that can stand well in times of pressure, joy, crisis, jubilation, need, thanksgiving. For me such prayers of inspiration include the following:

The most well-known prayer of Dag Hammarskjöld, former Secretary General of the United Nations:
"For all that has been — Thanks! To all that shall be — Yes!"

A prayer blossomed in the fertile ground of third-world poverty:
"For those who hunger, give them bread. And for those who have bread, give them a hunger for justice."

A prayer popularized by the Chaplain to the United States Senate, Presbyterian preacher Peter Marshall:
"Lord, where we are wrong, make us willing to change, and where we are right, make us easy to live with."

A prayer by Bishop W.E. Orchard that, while originating a century ago, still rings strong today:
"... and when the day goes hard, [and] cowards steal from the field, may our place be found where the fight is fiercest."

From that illustrious writer known as "Anonymous," a prayer considered central to the mission and vision of the Children's Defense Fund:
"Dear Lord, be good to the children. The sea is so wide, and their boats are so small."

Prayer by Martin Luther King, Jr., during his second year as pastor of Dexter Avenue Baptist Church, Montgomery, Alabama:
"Lord, help me to accept my tools. However dull they are, help me to accept them... then help me to set out to do what I can do with my tools."

"Pray For Me"

My friend Seymour dropped by my study at the church recently and inquired about a particular phrase common in most ecclesial settings but somewhat vexing to him.

"Well, Rev., I may be late to the party but I was wondering what it really means when people say, 'Please pray for me.' What's going on with all of that?" he asked as he leaned in the doorway and gazed directly at me.

"How did this come up, Seymour?' was my first rejoinder.

"Where haven't I heard it!" he said excitedly. "I hear it nearly everywhere in and around churches!"

I answered, with an attempt at thoroughness, "It's a customary, familiar way to ask for help, to express a concern for the spiritual welfare of another, and to seek a needed connection with a person, with a group, and with God."

Seymour wasn't satisfied with my answer. "And do you really pray for folks after they ask you to?"

"Sure," I said. "Absolutely."

"But do you only pray for folks — when they ask you?" Seymour continued with his interrogatives.

"No, of course not. I pray for folks in a number of ways, everyday, whether they ask for my prayers or not," I replied.

Seymour still wasn't satisfied. "Well, Rev., tell me about when and how you pray in response to prayer requests," he said, with a little incredulous edge in his voice.

"Normally," I said in a measured, normal tone of voice, "it goes like this. When someone asks me to pray for them, or for someone they know, or for a friend or a family member, or for a special circumstance in their lives or in the world, I begin praying silently right then. If someone calls me up at church or on my cell and asks for prayers, I either pray with them over the phone or start praying right after the phone call has ended. In the privacy of my study, or in my car, or at home, I've found that praying out loud is a rich experience of blessing."

"Out loud, really?" Seymour seemed to scoff.

"Sure," I said, "it's an embodied reaction to a sincere request. It prompts me to be accountable and responsive. And as I continue to pray for others in response to their prayer requests,

right then and later, whether silently or out loud, I discover a
bond of loving connection developing between the person who
requested the prayer and myself and God."

"Don't you get lost in all the prayer requests?" Seymour
queried.

"Hasn't happened yet. There's always time to pray. We can
usually do more than we ever imagined," I said.

Seymour pressed onward, "But aren't some of the prayer
requests over the top, asking for special privilege, divine
intervention, supernatural prerogative just for some people?"

"If you're asking if I pray for people to win the lottery," I
said, "or that God reverse the aging process, or that some folks
get an advantage while others lose out, no, I never pray like that.
And no one, yet, has ever asked for those kinds of prayers, at
least not in a serious vein. But everyone seeks the best possible
outcomes and has the highest hopes for those they treasure.
Instances of healing and course correction and saving insights
have graced countless people throughout history, and, I believe,
will continue to bless in mysterious ways countless folks in the
future."

"Maybe my question has more to do with what prayer
actually is," Seymour said in a quiet, calm tone. "What is prayer
all about, really?" he summed up his concern.

My reply was brief: "Well, my friend, that may take up way
more time than you or I have right now, but Ill offer this much.
Prayer is the soul's cry. It is the place and the time and the mood
and the moment in which God meets us. It is conversation and
communion with the Holy One. It is encounter with the
numinous. It is connection with the *mysterium tremendum*. Prayer
is, at once, the deepest need and the highest hope of humanity.
All prayers, even our bumbling ones, can be transformed into
true union with God. All prayers, even our struggling, hesitant,
ignorant, hobbled ones, are received by God."

"Well, OK, I suppose that'll have to do for now," Seymour
said with a sigh.

Then, as he left my study, he turned back and shot one final
comment over his shoulder: "And you'll pray for me, Rev.,
right? Not for special privilege or anything like that, but more in
that connecting way?"

"Absolutely, Seymour," I said, "I'm praying right now. And
I'll continue to pray for you."

A Prayer for July 4th

God of all ages, God of all places, God of all times and eternity,
Whose almighty hand has crafted and formed every people,
Whose gracious guidance has provided rare and profound
    opportunities for our own nation,
help us all to understand our celebrations this July 4th holiday.

Help us to remember how painfully our freedom was won,
the down-payment that was made for it,
the installments that have been proffered down the years
since the grand experiment known as the United States began.
Help us to know how freedom is to be more fully wrought
for all of Your children, here and elsewhere,
day by day by day.

Inspire us to see freedom not as the right to do as we please,
but as new occasions to please to do what is right and good.
Lead us, O God, so that our trust in You is not merely stamped
    upon our money
but expressed fully in our lives.

Help us to understand that liberty is made manifest best
by seeking Your will of peace and goodwill for one and all.
Give us courage to fend off all worldly fears,
especially the fear of standing in singular fashion for the rights
    of humanity,
since that is how we were born.

As we have been made prosperous,
    make us also good.
As we have been preserved in freedom,
    preserve us also by justice.
And, dear Lord of our Lives, as we have been kept free,
    will we now be kept true?
As we have become rich in things,
    will we now become richer still in principles and
    munificence?
We pray this prayer with fervent hope that we shall know Your
    truth and it shall truly set us free. AMEN

A Prayer Practice for Times When Prayer Is Hard

Pray
    but if you cannot pray ...
Speak
    but if you cannot speak ...
Listen
    but if you cannot listen ...
Read
    but if you cannot read ...
Look
    but if you cannot look ...
Imagine
    but if you cannot imagine ...
Hope
    but if you cannot hope ...
Think
    but if you cannot think ...
Cry out
    but if you cannot cry out ...
Reach out
    but if you cannot reach out ...
Cling to God
    but if you cannot cling to God ...
Cling to someone
    but if you cannot cling to someone ...
Whisper your need
    but if you cannot whisper your need ...
Pray
    and repeat this process until prayer comes more easily.

All Deaths Caused By Violence Are Tragic

All deaths caused by violence are tragic. But some of those deaths are more tragic than others.

On August 23, 2013, Myeisha Turner and her three-year-old daughter Damiah White were killed in their home in Kansas City. While some crimes of violence in the metro area have been resolved, the murders of Damiah and Myeisha have not. The assailant has not yet been found. It was a humbling (and daunting) experience to be part of a public witness calling on all people in the metro area to do all they can to bring an end to violence wherever we live. My part in that witness included the composition of the following prayer, which was shared in an array of congregations across the metro area, October 26, 2013.

A Prayer for Damiah White & Myeisha Turner

Giver of all Eternal Comfort,
as we continue to mourn the deaths of Damiah White and
     Myeisha Turner,
we pray for Your inspiration and wisdom.
Inspire each of us and all people everywhere in the metro area,
particularly in communities of faith,
with Your enthusing power
to not grow weary in well-doing,
to seek justice for little Damiah . . . and all other children,
to seek justice for Myeisha . . . and all other young mothers,
to secure the communities in which we dwell
and the homes in which we live
with righteousness and honesty and fervent care,
especially for those among us who are the most vulnerable.

Grant that we may bind ourselves together
with such purpose and persuasion and bonding,
heart to heart and soul to soul,
that respect will be accorded unto Damiah's memory
and honor unto Myeisha's memory,
and justice will prevail for them.

Hear our prayers, O God,
from the broken hearts of we who offer these prayers
on behalf of those who have known too much tragedy and
burdensome loss, as we participate in the sacred quest
of healing our city's heart,
and, indeed, the hearts of all cities everywhere

AMEN.

Giving Thanks

Thankful for so much and so many today:

- For the selfless largesse of previous generations;
- For the experience of grace and generosity in food pantries everywhere;
- For religious communities where the quest of faith — including all of its foundational affirmations and its necessary questions — can be fully engaged;
- For the tender care parents offer their children, and for children who reciprocate that care at the end of a parent's life;
- For the builders and dreamers and architects and carpenters and welders and painters and workers who have created and still create the places where we live and work and play;
- For friends, colleagues, associates, and acquaintances who enrich our lives with their unique personalities, particular perspectives, and divinely different talents;
- For those moments when someone holds our hands and comforts us, imparting hope to live beyond a current crisis or a pressing loss;
- For God's grand palette of colors in nature's cornucopia of beauty;
- For all the gracings of music — whether embodied in a Bruce Springsteen concert or a Mozart concerto or a Doc Watson guitar riff or church choir's anthem or Mahalia Jackson's witnessing tributes or Hank Williams' soulful crooning or an *a capella* group's swooning exultation or an eight-year-old's piano recital;
- For the gift of prayer and its portal to redemption;
- For sunsets that take our breath away;
- For the gift of forgiveness and its power to transform relationships;
- For firefighters and EMTs and police officers who save lives and protect communities and risk themselves in constant service;

- For the boundless gifts of words that can change dungeons into palaces, hurts into healing, isolation into communion, ignorance into illumination;
- For those who stand and sit and serve and love and care in the place of absent parents, grandparents, uncles, aunts;
- For food and people to share it with in joyful, humbling, deep satisfaction;
- For the Creator, Redeemer, and Sustainer who makes all gratitude possible.

Thankful for Dr. King's Prayers

On what would have been Dr. King's 85th birthday, and as we approach the annual celebration of the Martin Luther King, Jr. national holiday, I'm more and more appreciative of Professor Lewis Baldwin.

Dr. Baldwin deserves credit as the chief steward and premier champion for the sharing of Dr. King's prayer life, made finally accessible in his exemplary description and analyses in *Never to Leave Us Alone: The Prayer Life of Martin Luther King, Jr.*, and, subsequently, in his editing of King's actual extant prayers in *Thou, Dear God: Prayers that Open Hearts and Spirits*.

Though the prayers by King that have now been published are few (68), Baldwin has taken a monumental step in broadening the shared understanding of King's life and legacy. King's spirituality and his actual prayer practices are available for fresh study and discovery.

In his public prayers King often focused on the mode of petition, beseeching God for strength in times of trial and occasions portending adversity. In worship services, either at Ebenezer Baptist Church in Atlanta, Georgia, or other religious gatherings, he regularly prayed for social justice to be made manifestly real and vibrant. In times of great difficulty or uncertainty, he prayed for spiritual guidance, for himself and all others.

Among King's preferred prayers by others were those by Augustine, St. Francis of Assisi, John Bunyan, and George Whitefield, as well as the lyrics by hymn composers such as Isaac Watts. Frequently, at significant points in his public prayers and at the conclusion of pastoral prayers in church services, King would cite phrases of one or another of his favorite hymns and gospel songs.

In his prayers and his prayer practices, we see the sources of Martin Luther King's strength and the wellspring for his faith. When one considers the massive achievements King accomplished in his brief 39 years, it seems altogether reasonable and appropriate to claim that his prayer life was a primary foundational source that empowered his oratorical eloquence, his social activism commitments, and his spiritual leadership.

Rejoicing and Weeping and Resurrection (+Resources for Talking with Our Children About Tragedy)

The events at the beginning of Holy Week in the greater Kansas City area have given new meaning to the apostle Paul's mandate in the book of Romans: "Rejoice with those who rejoice, weep with those who weep."

Our Palm Sunday celebrations at Community were exceedingly jubilant, definitely a time to "rejoice with those who rejoice." The morning was a trifecta of joy. Those in attendance in our three services are likely to report that the musical proclamations they experienced on Palm Sunday were some of the best music ever heard on Music Sunday!

As I left church and headed toward my trusted Silver Streak to bear me home, I smiled at the site of the first dandelion of the season on the church lawn. I even stopped to take a picture of it for later posting on Facebook. "How silly," I thought, "that such a lovely little weed should have been given a name that means 'lion's tooth'!"

Little did any of us know that the greater Kansas City area would be caught in the teeth of ravaging hatred. How soon we shifted from Jesus' triumphant entry in Jerusalem on Palm Sunday to the Golgotha of Good Friday. How quickly we moved from rejoicing to weeping.

A lone gunman, Frazier Glenn Miller, perverted by prejudice, twisted by bigotry, consumed by hatred, killed Bill Corporon and his grandson Reat Underwood in the parking lot of the Jewish Community Center in Overland Park, Kansas, and Terri LeManno, an occupational therapist and mother of three, in the parking lot of Village Shalom, a senior living facility a few blocks away.

Miller, a known anti-Semite and white supremacist — with a depressingly long record of championing hatred and fomenting enmity in political campaigns — had obviously targeted two Jewish sites on the eve of Passover, one of the holiest times on the Jewish calendar. It is a sorrowful irony that Bill Corporon and Reat Underwood were Methodists and Terri LaMonna was Catholic.

In the wake of the tragedy, we moved from "rejoicing with those who rejoice" to "weeping with those who weep." Community members and I, along with countless others here and across the nation, immediately joined together in constant, consoling prayers for those touched, directly and indirectly, by the tragic deaths.

After being on the phone and in email contact with many friends throughout the metro area Sunday afternoon and evening, it was clear that our shared love and compassion are strong and abiding. It was equally clear that double portions of both will be needed as we proceed through the wake of these shocking losses. (Part of what will be needed is a sharpened ability to speak with our children about what has happened. In this regard, please see the resources listed at the end of this piece.**)

In helping to plan a communal interfaith Service of Unity and Hope, scheduled for Thursday, April 17, at the Jewish Community Center, I've been humbled and heartened by the extraordinary caring and tender sensitivity being shown by everyone. And I have been strongly emboldened to believe — with an unshakable confidence — that weeping will be transformed into greater mercy and deeper compassion.

A renewed resolve has also been quickened within many, including myself, that love, hope, and the bonds of community, infused with a keener sense of God's compassionate presence all along the way, will not only help us to endure but will empower us to prevail.

I am reminded by Jesus' exemplary forgiveness on the cross and his dealings with those who hated him that such resolve will also lead us to pray for Glen Miller and those like him that they might forever turn away from hatred.

By responding with love, grace, and solidarity against the tragic logic of violence, we make our shared journey toward Easter a truly "Holy Week."

We need Easter this year. We need the reminder that love triumphs over death. We need the recollection of God's grace, writ large in Christ's resurrection and our own. And we need each other.

Let us do our family members and all of our friends a favor this week and strongly encourage them to join us for Easter services. We have four glorious celebrations to choose from. I look forward to sharing my Easter sermon, "Living in the Land of 'Is'" with one and all, as we proclaim the sure and certain hope of the resurrection reality.

See you in church!

Love, Bob

P.S.

While the following resources aren't exhaustive, they will give families a start in talking about community tragedies.

From the National Institute of Mental Health re: What Community Members Can Do
http://infocenter.nimh.nih.gov/pdf/helping children and adolescents cope with violence and disasters what community members can do.pdf

From the National Institute of Mental Health re: What Parents Can Do
http://infocenter.nimh.nih.gov/pdf/helpingchildrenandadolesc entscopewithviolenceanddisasterswhatparentscando.pdf

Kaiser Foundation
http://www.talkwithkids.org/twkbookletviolence.pdf

Union of Reform Judaism
http://urj.org/life/family/bereavement/?syspage=article&item _id=98233

Adapted from the National Council of Churches and The Children's Defense Fund
http://www.ncccusa.org/nmu/mce/childrenterrorism.html

Service of Unity and Hope

Jewish Community Campus — White Theatre
5801 W 115th Street
Overland Park, Kansas
Thursday, April 17, 2014

It was a humbling and inspiring experience to participate in the Service of Unity and Hope held this morning, April 17, 2014, in the White Theatre at the Jewish Community Campus in Overland Park, Kansas. The service, attended by an overflow crowd of more than 1,300 people, was a compassionate and resolved response to the tragic deaths on Palm Sunday of William Corporon and Reat Underwood at JCC, and the death of Terri LaManno at Village Shalom, at the hands of a lone gunman known for his anti-Semitic and racist hatred. Everyone who participated in leadership roles — coordinated masterfully by Rabbi Art Nemitoff, and including powerful words and presence by Jacob Schreiber, U.S. Attorney General Eric Holder, Rev. Adam Hamilton, Fr. Charles Rowe, Rev. Glen Miles, and Matt Lewis, along with beautiful musical contributions by Rabbi Jeffrey Shron, Cantor Sharon Kohn, Hazzan Tahl BenYehuda, Millie Edwards and Tim Whitmer — contributed to an outstanding moment of hope and affirmation.

It was an honor to offer the following prayer as part of the service.

Prayer of Healing and Hope

Gracious God, Compassionate Creator of us all, Loving Lord
    who has no Lord,
we know that You are magnificently multilingual.
You hear all our prayers,
whether we recite the Kaddish
or say a Rosary
or intone Wesley's blessing for those who sleep forever within
    Your tender, eternal embrace.

You have heard our cries in the night: "This is not the way it's
    supposed to be!"
As we contend with what is, how thankful we are for Your
    wondrous love.
In the face of tragedy, You have loved every one of us as if there
    was only one of us to love.
How gladly we have held onto Your comfort in its many forms
    —
a whispered word of caring, the sharing of a meal, a note tinged
    with tears.

And in it all we have begun to see a path toward healing:
that the only way out of pain is through,
the only way beyond loss is through,
the only way to the light of healing is to go through this present
    darkness,
step by step, breath by breath, hand in hand,
stumbling maybe, from time to time, but always moving
    forward,
together, with one another and with You.

As healing moves among all of us here, and throughout the
    greater Kansas City community,
heal those whose minds have been blighted by bigotry,
whose hearts have been haunted by hatred,
whose souls have been perverted by prejudice,
that they might turn away forever from the evils of enmity and
    violence.
And strengthen our resolve to resist any and all malevolent ideas
    that fuel heinous acts.

We mourn, O God, but we do not mourn as those who have no
    hope.
Because of the sacrament of memory, a cornerstone for both
    Judaism and Christianity
(especially during this week of holy days) and for the adherents
    of every faith,
we have recalled the blessed lives gone too soon,
and thus we know we can endure, we must endure for the sake
    of their legacies.

Lift our hearts with the gift of hope, O God, and we will prevail.
Lift our eyes to new horizons, O God, until we are emboldened
    to believe
that beyond the valley of the shadow of death
goodness and mercy will surely follow us all the days of our
    lives.

In Your powerful and precious name we pray, Amen.

NOTES
No one ever writes or prays without the infusion of umpteen sources.
The following informed this prayer:

"... who sleep forever within Your tender, eternal embrace." A variation
of a phrase by John Wesley, the founder of Methodism, in his "Prayer
for the Dead" — "...who sleep in Thee."

"...You have loved every one of us as if there was only one of us to
love." A phrase by St. Augustine.

"... the only way out is through..." I am indebted to The Rev. Dr. Johnny
Ray Youngblood, who shared a form of this trope with me at St. Paul
Community Baptist Church, in Brooklyn, New York, September 2001. A
precedent can also be found in Robert Frost's poem, "A Servant to
Servants," which includes the line, "The best way out is always
through."

"... we do not mourn as those who have no hope." See I Thessalonians
4:13 in the New Testament.

" ...especially during this week of holy days..." The day of this service,
April 17, 2014, marked the fourth day since the beginning of Judaism's
observance of Passover and the very day of Christianity's Maundy
Thursday observance.

"...beyond the valley of the shadow of death goodness and mercy will
surely follow us all the days of our lives" — from Psalm 23.

RESISTING HARMFUL RELIGION

Resisting Harmful Religion

Recently a strife-mongering radio commentator has opined an idiotic thesis. (I'd rather not mention his name here in this space but will certainly tell you, if you ask. I think it's normally best to avoid unseemly rhetoric.) According to this commentator, the current Ebola outbreak in Africa, and its presence in two cases of infected health care workers now in the U.S., might be a divinely authored method for solving what he perceives to be America's problems.

I want to say clearly and strongly here, as I have stated on numerous occasions before, that such prejudiced commentary masquerading as religious sentiment is not worthy of Christianity nor any other religious tradition. Such commentary is, at best, woefully uninformed and recklessly thoughtless, and at worst, willfully stupid. Such thinking participates in what I call God-is-a-big-mean-monster theology, latching on to health crises (or natural disasters or war-torn areas of the world or current-event controversies) and attaching God's condemnation to them. In the process, they give Christ and anyone who follows Christ a bad name.

Contrast such unfortunate opinions with the commendable humility and equanimity of Dr. Kent Brantley, one of the two Americans who were infected with the Ebola virus and now are under care in Atlanta. When he was infected, Dr. Brantley was in Liberia with his wife Amber and their two children to serve a two-year fellowship in a residency program of Samaritan's Purse, a Christian relief charity.

Last Friday Dr. Brantley issued a statement which illuminated his exemplary character: "I thank God for His mercy as I have wrestled with this terrible disease. I also want to extend my deep and sincere thanks to all of you who have been praying for my recovery as well as for Nancy [Writebol, the other American infected with the Ebola virus, also under care in Atlanta] and for the people of Liberia and West Africa." Beyond the prayers which so many have prayed for his and Nancy's recovery, Dr. Brantley expressed his hope that "God will give me everything I need to be faithful to Him."

In addition to appreciating Dr. Brantley's inspiring attitude,

I think there are a few other things we can do when vile statements are made in the name of faith.

- When we hear or see or otherwise witness ridiculous statements in connection to God, we can stand up and say, "Wait a minute, that's not right. The God I worship has nothing to do with punishing anyone with disease or disaster."
- Pray that persons issuing hurtful and harmful statements will come to their senses and live more into the image of God in which they were created. It's not enough to simply express outrage at hateful speech. We are called to pray for the transformation of those issuing the vitriolic words.
- Let one and all do their homework and exercise their fullest mental capacities to get to a common set of facts, including the extraordinary science that truly is of God and is being used for the healing and health of those who are hurting.

Let's not be silent when seemingly crazy utterances smear God's reputation and ours as people of faith. But let us also keep in mind the high example of Dr. Brantley's demeanor as a solid standard for our conduct and engagement with the issues.

Living Faithfully, Beyond May 21, 2011

Harold Camping's now famous prediction of the end of the world on May 21, 2011, is at once misguided, regrettable, sad, and dangerous.

His so-called calculations are obviously misguided, and his claims of scriptural insight and special revelation don't align with the Bible in any way. Scripture consistently warns against anyone ever knowing the absolute times when God will or will not act in our daily lives or in momentous historic occasions. (See Mark 13:32, Matthew 24:36, and Acts 1:7, for examples.)

His predictions are regrettable, since he and we all have so much more important work to do. And there are so many more important discussions to share, like how to improve our education systems and provide adequate nutrition for all children and youth.

Camping's so-called prognostications are sad in that they flatten the human enterprise to an ignoble and base level: rabid concern about the spectacle of an apocalyptic end of all things. This may be the most egregious aspect of what he is doing: portraying God as a vengeful, waste-laying, fear-inducing, world-destroying deity. His understanding of God is light-years away from the God of love and mercy proclaimed in and by Jesus of Nazareth. I find that his forecastings are more like previews of shock-and-scare slasher movies rather than caring proclamations of the Creator of the Universe moving the earth toward consummation.

Ultimately, Camping's peculiar anticipations of what will happen on May 21, 2011, are dangerous in that they are leading unwitting, trusting souls to what are likely to be a series of torturous faith crises.

When we, the Left Behind, gather for worship at Community on Sunday morning, May 22, let us offer a prayer for Harold Camping and those who follow him that they will not lose their faith because the world has continued beyond the day he predicted its end. I offer this invitation not with the certainty of crystal-clear clairvoyance, but trusting in a God whose ways are above and beyond anything any human being can ever predict.

Always with hope — see you in church!

Letter re: Mr. Terry Jones

(The following is a response to a question posed by Tony, a Community member,
about the furor fomented by Terry Jones down in Gainesville, Florida, as he
plans to burn copies of the Quran on Sat., Sept. 11th. With Tony's endorsement, a
portion of the letter, in an expanded form, is shared here to promote tolerance
and good will in a time too much torn asunder by enmity and hatred.)

Thursday, Sept. 9, 2010

Dear Tony,

Many thanks for your graciously kind note. It's always good
and right to bring up questions about important matters related
to our faith.

This coming Sunday, Sept. 12, during a brief moment in my
sermon, I'll have some more to say about Mr. Jones and his
yearning to burn copies of the Quran. For now, part of my
response to your question is contained in a television interview I
did with a reporter from KSHB (Channel 41) about an hour
before the Agape Feast. A snippet of my remarks is contained in
the story which aired last night on their 10 pm news:
        http://www.nbcactionnews.com/dpp/news/local_news/kansascitycongr
egationsreacttopastor%E2%80%99sbookburning
While I had heard (back in July or August) about Mr. Jones'
plan to burn copies of the Quran, I still don't know many details
about him or his church. What I've discerned from the public
comments he has made and from his website is that he espouses
a kind of reactionary fundamentalism that condemns folks who
don't think and believe as he does. What he is promoting and
doing to register his protest against people he thinks are his
enemies is mostly bigotry and purely founded on hatred.

Such bigotry is borne out of a willful ignorance which
thoughtful people everywhere, and especially Christians in the
U.S., need to resist. Because of the freedom of religion we enjoy
in this country, he has every right to be as willfully ignorant and
bigoted and full of hatred as he chooses.

But it behooves thoughtful people — and, here, I like to
think of Community as a gathering of such thoughtful people —
to say privately among our friends and to declare as publicly as
we can that his choices, and the choices of those who follow him,

are sad, regrettable, and, indeed, repugnant.

Mr. Jones' proposed actions of burning Qurans will only incite a media blitz in this country and further inflame the small-focused passions of a small band of equally bigoted, hate-filled fundamentalistic Muslims. And none of that can be good for the world.

As I said in a portion of the television interview (which ended up on the cutting room floor), Mr. Jones represents to the world the worst possible face of the Christian faith and the worst possible example of a U.S. citizen. From all we know about the person, witness, and ministry of Jesus of Nazareth, Mr. Jones stands totally outside of what is acceptably Christian. And from what we continue to learn from Christ's ongoing presence and God's persistent love of the human family, Mr. Jones' proposed actions on the 9th anniversary of 9/11 would do nothing to honor the tragic victims connected to that infamous day and would very likely put yet more people, particularly American soldiers, in harm's way.

We best express the faith we hold dear and true when we live out its highest principles and not by committing violent actions against the objects/symbols of another faith. While the Quran is not holy to Christians in the way that the Bible is for us, it is not up to Mr. Jones to determine what is holy and what is not. Holiness is never contained solely in a book. Holiness is ultimately a never-ending project for the living of our days. We don't make ourselves "right" by condemning others (and the things they hold dear) as wrong. We become "right" as we do all that we can to embody love in the world, day by day, step by step, breath by breath.

In this regard, perhaps what we can do best to embody the love called for by our faith is to pray for Mr. Jones, and those who follow his belligerently hate-filled counsel, and try to imagine how he might be transformed out of his hatred and away from his fearful posture toward others. How we might participate in that transformation, and our own, toward a more respectful and civil engagement with the important issues of the day must also be part of our prayers as well.

Those are a few of my thoughts in response to your wonderful note and questions. Keep asking them!

Love, Bob

About Fred Phelps' Passing

This week my friend Seymour dropped by my study at church to see if I had heard about the death of Fred Phelps. Phelps, as many if not all of us in the greater Kansas City area know, was a vitriolic proponent of a scourging version of religion for nearly 60 years.

I said that indeed I had heard the news. Seymour also asked if I had heard that he'd been excommunicated from the very Westboro group he founded in Topeka, Kansas. I allowed that I had heard that strange news, too.

Seymour remembered that Community was the first Kansas City congregation assaulted by Fred Phelps' venom, when his group protested the funeral service of Kevin Oldham, a Community member, an extraordinarily gifted pianist, a brilliant composer, the treasured brother of Leslie Oldham, and the beloved son of Barbara and Bill Oldham, our choir director at the time. I remembered how much pain and anguish Phelps and his group had caused the Oldhams and Community's church family.

"I heard that you and a clergy colleague went over to Topeka to ask him not to stage the protest. Is that right?" Seymour continued in his interlocutor's ways.

"Yes, we did. Bob Cueni and I drove over to Topeka — on the Wednesday of Holy Week, if memory serves — and sought to live out what Jesus recommends in Matthew's gospel," I recollected.

"And what does Jesus recommend in Matthew's gospel, anyway?" Seymour asked.

"Well, Seymour, that you seek a peaceful, civil redress for a wrong done against you by another. We went to the front door of Phelps' compound to ask him to stop what he was saying about Kevin, about his parents, and about Community, and not to protest the funeral. But it didn't work. They came any way."

"When the protest happened on the day of the funeral, I heard that Community members served Lamar's donuts to the Phelps group. That's right, isn't it?" Seymour asked.

"Yes," I replied, "it was one of our finest hours as a congregation, I believe. We thought we ought to do what Jesus might have done. Phelps galvanized the compassion and unity of our church family more solidly than almost anything I'd ever seen at Community."

"Wasn't there a Kansas City, Missouri, ordinance put in place, disallowing the protesting of funerals during certain times before and after the time of the funerals?" Seymour went on.

"Yes, Katherine Shields introduced the ordinance and several of us testified at City Hall about its appropriateness," I recalled. "But a statement by a Community member haunted me then and challenges me still today," I continued. "She said, 'You know, Bob, even after the ordinance passes, the hate will still be there.'"

Seymour kept querying, "What now, in the wake of his death?"

"It's hard to say, Seymour," I answered. "Pity, for the most part, I think. And prayers that, at the end, he might have experienced an epiphany about the sad, destructive folly of his fear-based way of life. And continuing prayers and advocacy for those who were the object of his enmity. And abiding prayers for his family and any followers who have been infected with his perversion of what it means to be religious."

Then Seymour said something as true as the sky is blue on a perfect opening day out at Kauffman Stadium: "Well, there's one thing I know for sure: if you hate him back, as he hated so many, his way wins. But if you love..." At this, Seymour's voice trailed off, and he seemed to be looking somewhere far in the future. And then he smiled big and said, "And if you love... love always wins."

About Osama bin Laden's Death

The news came in a flash Sunday evening, and most of us have hardly had time enough to adjust to the seemingly surreal revelation by President Obama that Osama bin Laden is dead. The death of bin Laden brings to partial closure a long and painful chapter in the struggle against terrorism.

Our responses to this news are natural and multitudinous: pride in the military's success in fulfilling a mission; gladness that one of the premier princes of evildoing has been halted; relief that one who had caused unfathomable heartache will no longer give orders to cause further heartache; dazed benumbing in the face of the ongoing conundrum of terrorism; fearful uncertainty because stopping one individual does not eradicate a cabal of hatred; rueful resignation because the death of bin Laden does not bring back to life even one person among those lost on September 11, 2001, or among the thousands who have died in Iraq and Afghanistan; puzzlement and inner conflict because killing and death are ultimately antithetical to the essence of the Judeo-Christian heritage. This is an emotionally complicated moment.

Which is not unlike most of our other moments. Three things are for sure, it seems to me, in all moments:

(1) One response we all can make is to be prayerful, even more prayerful than we have been over the past nine and a half years. "We are as we pray," I have said to many who have asked what to do in such circumstances. Communications with our Maker, Redeemer, and Sustainer are always in order, and never more so that in an emotionally complicated time.

(2) We also can remember. Frederick Buechner's guidance is consistently wise: memory is one of the most sacred acts of the human community. Let us remember the precious lives that have been lost and the precious lives that we enjoy now. Let us remember the families who lost loved ones in London and Tanzania and Kenya and elsewhere because of bin Laden's orders, spanning two decades. Let us remember the valiant vigilance of those who put themselves in harm's way to contain and control terrorism's merciless mayhem. Let us remember all the children and how we are to protect them so that they can

have a future.

(3) We can dig deep into our faith, with caution and reserve and humility. Our faith teaches us that we can never revel in death or killing. At least not in Jesus' name, not in the name of the Prince of Peace. We are people of life-giving faith and proponents of healing and the possibilities of loving forgiveness, even of enemies. Am I glad that bin Laden has been stopped? Yes. Am I thankful for the care of our nation's armed forces? Yes. Am I relieved that one of the most heinous evildoers in the course of my lifetime has been relegated to the ignominy he deserves? Absolutely. Yet and still, I am called, as I believe all Christians are called, to plumb the rich depths of Jesus' way of life and love for the ultimate answers to life's most perplexing challenges. And in this regard I know that bin Laden's death will not finally stymie the hatred of those whose twisted version of Islam compels them to continue their murderous ways.

As Martin Luther King, Jr. keenly noted, "The ultimate weakness of violence is that it is a descending spiral, begetting the very thing it seeks to destroy. Instead of diminishing evil, it multiplies it... Darkness cannot drive out darkness: only light can do that. Hate cannot drive out hate: only love can do that."

So, I will pray and remember and dig deep into faith. And I encourage you to do the same. We are not done with the troubling travail of terrorism. For a moment we have reason to take a breath. May it be a breath imbued by the Spirit of God who will inspire us to transform the world so that terrorism is unthinkable and killing no longer drives the story of our fragile humanity's search for peace.

(This piece was shared during Community's Wednesday evening chapel service on May 4, 2011.)

TRIBUTES, REMEMBRANCES, & APPRECIATIONS

Appreciations

Are there places, persons, moments, or things that are less appreciated than you think they should be? Try listing them and sharing with friends. While our lists might be different in emphasis and intent, surely a sharing can inspire deeper appreciation. Here's my provisional list:

- letter carriers who deliver the mail;
- a dove's cooing in the morning;
- the way rain and sun tango together in a summertime tomato patch;
- a surgeon who can quote poetry;
- a poet who loves to cook Thanksgiving dinner;
- clothbound hardcover books;
- the grace of a clean bill of health;
- the availability of pavement, no matter its state of repair or disrepair, nearly everywhere you need to go in the U.S.;
- gravel roads that stream along the edges of verdant fields;
- the luxury of a glass of cool water;
- the value of a 98 mph fastball;
- a first-grader's anticipation of the first day of school;
- worms in good soil;
- the sound of a violin played by a master violinist;
- the music made on a piano by a ten-year-old virtuoso;
- the prayers others pray for you without you ever knowing it;
- the accommodation and collaboration among Jews, Christians and Muslims in the Andalusian world in the Middle Ages.

I look forward to seeing your lists!

Tribute for Judy Hellman at 2014 MORE² Banquet

I have known Judy Hellman now for a quarter century and my only regret in our friendship is that it did not begin sooner. Had I known Judy sooner, earlier — say, when she was in kindergarten — I would have surely seen her on the playground as a justice champion at the tetherball pole when somebody rudely cut in line, or defending those who were preyed upon and put down in the classroom because they were different. As it is, I've still seen plenty of what makes Judy one of the great champions for justice, for goodness, and for what her religious tradition calls *hesed.*

Judy is like unto the iconic figure of Tom Joad in the novel *The Grapes of Wrath.* Toward the end of John Steinbeck's masterpiece about the ravages of dustbowl poverty, Joad proclaims a clarion-clear commitment to be everywhere his mother is, everywhere there's a righteous struggle, everywhere there's a good fight going on for the poor and the hungry and the dispossessed.

Well Judy Hellman, you've been all around, and you've been there!

Wherever there's a fight —
so hungry people can eat,
so eager children can learn,
so caring citizens can reduce violence in their neighborhoods,
so people can fulfill their dreams of racial and economic equity,
whether through MORE², or the JCRBAJC, or SCLC, or the NAACP, or
any of the umpteen other alphabet soup organizations you're involved in which fight vigilantly for justice.

And we know you will continue to be there —
in the way children laugh with delight
because their future prospects are prized more
than profits,
in the way parents beam with pride
because proper health care has been secured for

                    their families,
          in the way that folks shine after they've paid their debt to
    society
                    because they've been given a new lease on life
                    through a full return to the community,
          in the way that congregations stride forth in victory through
    MORE²
                    because they know the purpose of racial and
                    economic equity is clear and right.

          We thank you, Judy Hellman, for being there and for being
    here! It is a deeply gratifying privilege and a high honor to
    present you with MORE²'s 2014 Equity Partner Award.

Thomas Merton's Birthday

On what would have been his 100th birthday, January 31, 2015, it's good to remember Thomas Merton.

Among American Catholics, few figures loom larger than Thomas Merton when it comes to describing a "Great Soul" knowledgeable and authentic about prayer. Among American Catholics who rose to prominence in the 20th century, few have experienced a more lasting literary popularity than Thomas Merton. Among all American Christians, fewer still have had a greater impact on the conjoining of social justice and spiritual concerns than Thomas Merton.

In death as in life, Merton remains an enrapturing study of clashing contrasts. He was a monk who treasured solitude, and yet he became famous and attracted intellectual luminaries, civil rights workers, and popular culture celebrities to his hermitage at Our Lady of Gethsemani monastery, Bardstown, Kentucky.

His works on prayer are some of the most compelling ever written in English, and yet he is equally eloquent regarding issues of nuclear disarmament and eradicating world hunger.

His premier devotion was to God, and yet he loved the good gifts of God's world deeply.

He was a Catholic monk, and yet he was globally catholic in his yearning to learn about prayer from all religious traditions.

While singular in his genius and solitary in his devotional practice, Merton was always a part of a community. His entry into the monastic life was a move toward a greater togetherness with others, his brother monks. His time as a hermit during the last three years of his life would lead him to be connected with the wider reaches of the human family and a decisive journey to Thailand. He always had the hope of a keener unity within community and among all groups.

While we might yearn for radical, rational clarity about life, the world, our faith, and all kinds of other things, Merton viewed the spiritual practices of prayer and contemplation as pathways to the mysterious heart of God. Love — for God, for God's creation, for neighbors, for oneself in the embrace of God's love of the world — was Merton's central concern in so many of the prayers he composed for public use and in his own personal devotions. Always the intent was not focused on the self, but on how to give back to God.

Merton understood humility to be a crucial and necessary virtue to enact if one wants to be close to God. In fact, without humility, Merton held, we cannot even begin to know God's essential nature nor understand who we truly are as human beings. By becoming humble, we gain access to the possibility of true joy.

Merton was obviously a reformer — within his own monastic tradition, within the Catholic Church, and, through his correspondence and his books, within an ever-widening arc of ecumenical connections. Always within his vision was the concern for the new: "If our prayer is the expression of a deep and grace-inspired desire for newness of life — and not the mere blind attachment to what has always been familiar and 'safe' — God will act in us and through us..."

Thanks for Don Schutt

During the 2013 General Assembly of the Christian Church (Disciples of Christ) held in Orlando, Florida, participants in the Bethany Fellows took time to gather for a time of fellowship and celebration. The Bethany Fellowships help newly ordained pastors make the transition from seminary into sustained congregational ministry. The focus of the fellowships is on individual mentoring, peer accountability, expanding spiritual disciplines, and learning the best ministry practices. For me it has been a wonder-filled privilege and extraordinary grace to be a member of the leadership team for the Bethany Fellows.

Part of the Bethany Fellows celebration included a tribute to Don Schutt, the founding Executive Director. Don not only commands respect but inspires deep affection and fond regard among pastors in their twenties and thirties. And also among pastors in their forties, fifties, sixties, seventies, eighties, and ... !! One may ask, "Why?" Because Don is a player and a prayer.

Don Schutt is surely a player! He plays hard at the game of golf — to win, of course, but also to be better and to keep fit and to release tension and to be free, existentially free, for an afternoon or a morning at least, and because "it gives God pleasure." He plays hard for Habitat for Humanity by building houses every year. He plays hard for family, especially his wife and his sons and their families and his grandchildren. He plays hard for the children and the adults he tends to in his chaplaincy work. Don's a player!

Don is also an exemplary pray-er. The times I and countless others have asked Don to pray for a specific situation or circumstance or person or group are too numerous to count. As Thomas Merton and the rest of his brothers prayed for others at their Gethsemani monastery in Kentucky — and thereby, to use Merton's description, "held the world together by their prayers" — so Don Schutt has done for untold numbers of pastors and congregations.

"Lord, Teach Us to Pray" was the theme of the 2013 General Assembly. The Bethany Fellows know this theme well. They are on intimate terms with the motivation for the disciple's first request of Jesus for instruction. For all Christians this abides as an essential request, a basic, foundational need. For the Bethany Fellows and for an endless line of Don Schutt's friends, there is a second request like unto it: "Don, pray for us." And there are further sentiments that can be summed up with simple words of gratitude: "Don, thanks for praying for us and for teaching us how to pray better and more fully and with greater love."

Thank You, Joseph Siry!
Beth Sholom Congregation: Frank Lloyd Wright and Modern Religious Architecture

At long last, Joseph Siry's book on Frank Lloyd Wright's religious architecture has arrived. *Beth Sholom Congregation: Frank Lloyd Wright and Modern Religious Architecture* (University of Chicago Press) came in the mail this week, compliments of Mr. Siry, in gratitude for the help he received during his research efforts in Kansas City five-and-a-half years ago. And we are grateful indeed to Mr. Siry, professor of art history and American studies at Wesleyan University in Middletown, Connecticut, for his extraordinary and beautiful book.

This newest assessment of Frank Lloyd Wright's luminous legacy, stretching 705 pages and containing 300 illustrations and photographs, is worthy of the highest awards for architectural history books. The Beth Sholom Congregation in Philadelphia has now been put on the map for as long as there are readers and aficionados of architecture, religious or otherwise. While the Beth Sholom family of faith has been justifiably glad for its association with Frank Lloyd Wright (ever since its building opened in 1959), it now enters a new phase of pride with the publication of this book, which spans the broad reach of Wright's 70-year architectural career.

Community, too, can be glad and proud, because there is in the middle of Mr. Siry's brilliant book an entire chapter about Community's sanctuary building. In the course of the 52 pages devoted to Community, Mr. Siry provides the best and most comprehensive assessment of our unique church structure to date and much, much more, including:

- the history that preceded and surrounded the construction of our buildings throughout our congregational history;
- Community's place in the Disciples of Christ denomination and within the context of Kansas City's development;
- the significance of Dr. Burris Jenkins as Community's

pastor and as a civic leader;
- a history of progressive religion in Kansas City over the course of the first half of the 20th century;
- Wright's legitimation of his designs for Community, its eventual construction, and his association with it;
- the location of Community in Wright's catalogue of religious and theater buildings;
- and a detailed review of the Steeple of Light.

Mr. Siry's research appears absolutely exhaustive, exhuming and assaying more information than anyone knew was available.

Thank You, Galway Kinnell

Last week, during the glorious hubbub of the sixth game of the World Series, a moment full of great and grand emotions that I will not soon forget, Galway Kinnell, one of my favorite poets, breathed his last.

Winner of both a Pulitzer Prize and a National Book Award, he had endured a battle with leukemia, and died at home in Sheffield, Vermont, at the age of 87. Among his most famous books is *The Avenue Bearing the Initial of Christ into the New World*, which, along with all of his other books, is still in print.

Interestingly, W.S. Merwin, another of America's great poets, was his college roommate.

Kinnell was an extraordinary master of the English language and a wise guide for us in contemporary times. Witness the keen insight he had about his own role while he was with us: "To me poetry is somebody standing up, so to speak, and saying, with as little concealment as possible, what it is for him or her to be on earth at this moment."

Thank You, B'nai Jehudah — Celebrating 75 years of Congregational Friendship

Seventy-five years ago this month, on Halloween night, 1939, Community's former building at the corner of Linwood Boulevard and Forest Avenue burned to the ground. The beautiful Spanish Renaissance architecture of the much-used facility — a building that, like our own today, was put to maximum usage each and every day, but particularly on Sundays — was rendered into a pile of ash and smoldering cinders. The only thing salvaged, and miraculously so, were the membership records which Church Secretary Margaret Lamar rescued in the midst of the fire.

Less than a day or so had passed when the congregation of The Temple, Congregation B'nai Jehudah, led by Rabbi Samuel Mayerburg, offered its own sanctuary, at the corner of Linwood and Flora, to be the worshiping space for Community's congregation. A short week later, Community's membership, led by our senior minister, Dr. Burris Jenkins, voted to accept B'nai Jehudah's offer. For nearly a year, Community members and leaders enjoyed the gracious hospitality of B'nai Jehudah's members and leaders. The rest, as they say, is history.

Nearly 28 years ago, I had the good fortune to meet one of Rabbi Mayerburg's successors. His name? Michael Zedek. Rabbi Zedek was of utmost help and support, especially as we shared a similar clergy journey. Later, we would revel in the revival of our two congregations' long and enjoyable relationship. In time — years chockfull of numberless cups of coffee, ongoing passionate debates, shared communitywide projects, and a radio show's worth of fun and religious foment and fervor — Michael eventually became one of my dearest and most trusted friends. And the rest, as they say, is history.

Rabbi Arthur Nemitoff, one of Michael's successors, and I also became good friends after he was called to be senior rabbi at B'nai Jehudah in 2003. At the beginning of this millennium, as B'nai Jehudah experienced their own transitions with building and clergy, Community attempted to repay our debt from 1939 by opening our building and welcoming B'nai Jehudah to hold educational, social, and cultural events in our Activities Center. Rabbi Nemitoff and I have been on interfaith panels together, traveled to Israel together, shared in relief efforts for those adversely affected by Hurricane Katrina, led movie discussions together. Most recently, I was honored to assist Art on the public memorial service in the wake of the tragic shootings at the Jewish Community Campus and at Village Shalom. And the rest, as they say, is history.

Because of the auspicious anniversary of the burning of Community's former facility on Linwood and Forest, and because of B'nai Jehudah's overwhelming hospitality in response to our dire need in those years of changes, 1939-1940, and because of the friendship I've enjoyed with Rabbi Nemitoff, it seemed most appropriate to share our thanks with B'nai Jehudah.

Thus, Rabbi Nemitoff and I have arranged a pulpit exchange, the first half of which will take place on Friday, October 24, at 6:00 p.m., when I have been invited to speak during B'nai Jehudah's Sabbath services at 12320 Nall Ave, Overland Park, KS 66209. Because of our beloved Royals' World Series game that evening, I can assure that my sermon won't be overly long!

On Sunday, October 26, Rabbi Nemitoff will speak on "And You Shall Be a Blessing" at 10:45 a.m. in Community's sanctuary. The rest, as they might say, will be history-in-the-making.

I look forward to sharing these special services with Rabbi Nemitoff and participating in B'nai Jehudah's services. The exchange will be a wonderful occasion of enthusiastic thanksgiving and grand rejoicing. Let us all say our thanks to B'nai Jehudah's gracious congregation for their holy welcome and abiding affirmation. See you in church... and at B'nai Jehudah!

Remembering K. David Cole

People said they could listen to him speak for as long as he had breath. And, with deep and abiding appreciation, we did. On Tuesday afternoon, January 7, 2002, in a Los Angeles area hospital, The Rev. Dr. K. David Cole joined the Saints Triumphant, after a valiant and extended struggle with cancer.

David, as he was known far and wide to his friends, was Senior Minister Emeritus of the Swope Parkway United Christian Church here in Kansas City, Missouri, former Moderator of the Christian Church (Disciples of Christ) in the United States and Canada, and the recipient of numerous honorary degrees from institutions of higher education across the country. He was the namesake for the newly opened K. David Cole Place, sponsored locally by Swope Parkway United Christian Church and our Disciples National Benevolent Association. He was the very first recipient of the local Disciples Peace Fellowship chapter's "Peacemaker" award. He was one of the most celebrated and honored guest speakers at Regional Assemblies in the entire history of our denomination.

When you heard him preach, you heard his mind turning with great effect and his soul bounding forth with great passion. At the bedside he was an exemplary shepherd. At the communion table he was always the harbinger of a great reconciliation. In his study he constantly served with "a bishop's ear," a counselor of an exceeding comfort.

And when he spoke with that deep resonance that was his alone, he spoke not of himself nor of his own yearnings but of a great and conquering grace which God tendered to the world through Jesus Christ. At committee meetings, in the quiet of hallway counsel, in a car-trip conversation, and in his pulpit proclamations, it was always Christ and Christ's ways of love and hope and welcome that he proclaimed.

I will never forget his voice. He speaks to me even now, through his abiding spirit and precious memory. I knew David ever since he was my camp counselor in the days of my Texas youth. He was always one to turn to for a listening ear. David's steady strength and indefatigable patience made lasting impressions on countless ministers-to-be, including me. One of the great, reassuring pleasures for me in coming to Community was the knowledge that David was already here in Kansas City at the Swope Parkway United congregation. In time, we would share an exchange of pulpits, unceasing stories, numberless meals, and the accruals of a deep friendship. After a year's worth of intentional monthly meetings in 1996, David and I were graced to help create Christians Offering Love to Overcome Racism (C.O.L.O.R.s), a joint effort between Swope Parkway United and Community that has been enjoyed by our two congregations and celebrated in the media for more than 6 years. The wonderful fellowship which C.O.L.O.R.s shared last June during our Juneteenth observance is a testimony to David's lasting imprint on us all.

News releases about David's passing will be necessarily long and lovingly detailed. Plans for his services are still pending. We shall continue to pray and rejoice at the conclusion of David's rich and illustrious life, as it is celebrated in Los Angeles, where he and his wife Vi moved in retirement to be with family, and also here in Kansas, where his family of faith remains. And we will affirm again and again: in his resurrection to new life, as in life among us, he was and is "beloved."

Remembering the Rev. Dr. William Sloane Coffin, Jr., April 13, 2006

Bill Coffin died on Tuesday, April 12, 2006. And the mode of his passing was so very right: in the middle of the holiest week on the Christian calendar, basking in the sunshine in the backyard of his home in Strafford, Vermont, surrounded by family and friends. His body had finally relented to the congestive heart failure he had battled for years, but his soul was now enlarged to greet and embrace other great souls of the ages.

In my experience of exemplars, few better embodied that challenging ideal set forth by William Edwin Orchard: "And when the day goes hard, [and] cowards steal from the field... may our place be found where the fight is fiercest."

William Sloane Coffin, Jr. was "to the manor born" in New York City, yet the arc of his life would lead him, willingly and gladly, to encounter all manner of human existence in a journey of enthralling contrasts. He trained as a concert pianist, and he volunteered for military service in two wars. He worked for the Central Intelligence Agency on Russian affairs, and he sat at the feet of the world's greatest theologians as he prepared for the vocation of ministry. He became chaplain at Yale University, and he expressed the height of his homiletical powers as pastor of Riverside Church. He helped to galvanize awareness of the civil rights struggle as one of eleven Freedom Riders who ventured to Montgomery, Alabama, and he wrote, mused and prayed in his final home in rural Vermont. Yes, Coffin's was a life of enthralling contrasts.

In his expression of opinions and his public ministries, he was no stranger to controversy, and yet his warmth, charm and basic positive regard for all persons would eventually earn him respect even from those who didn't share one iota of his positions.

Warren Goldstein's superb biographical account of Coffin's life get's it just right, as he assesses Coffin's preaching and integrity as being prophetic and inspiring and always in touch with his times over the full course of his 40-year ministerial career. Coffin was both frustrated and energized by a 'holy impatience' with anything that did not comport with God's great love for all people.

Poet Edward Arlington Robinson once described the human enterprise as "a kind of spiritual kindergarten in which millions of befuddled infants are trying to spell God with the wrong blocks." Throughout his public ministry, Bill Coffin led countless persons — willing and unwilling, infants and oldsters — to spell "God" with more of the right blocks:

- at Yale University with his prophetic witness to students, faculty, administrators, alums, and the nation as a whole;
- at Riverside Church, with his daring vision and powerful preaching, beginning in the gorgeous Gotham of New York City, but always going beyond to a wider congregation;
- in his championing of the causes of the poor, the powerless, and the nuclear freeze movement, with that inimitable luster of leadership he lent so generously.

Indeed, Coffin was always priming countless folks to participate in a more humane, a more faithful "spelling bee."

The author of seven books, the two most recent ones being the award-winning *Credo* and *Letters to a Young Doubter*, Coffin came to embody the most noble elements of the Judeo-Christian tradition, always and ever bearing in his demeanor an effusive graciousness.

In my encounters with Bill Coffin, he consistently manifested a signal virtue: an exemplary capacity to share his compassionate, caring heart with others, on real terms and in real time. In short, he cared. He cared about people. He cared about people who cared. He cared about people who cared about others who cared about them.

And how can anyone who knew him, read his books, or heard him speak ever forget his wondrous ways with words?

In the estimation of many, one of the most powerful sermons he ever preached occurred on Sunday, January 23, 1983, while he was serving as the senior pastor of Riverside Church. In *"Alex's Death"* he eulogized his son Alex with his usual rhetorical flair for just the right words at just the right time, declaring that even though his son had "beat [him] to the grave," all of God's children are "under the Mercy."

Bill Coffin is now under the Mercy in a new, unfathomably

full dimension. So may we all be, as we recollect his life and give thanks to God for his legacy.

Remembering Jack Sullivan

Week before last, Tim Sullivan, a best friend from high school days, called twice. He first called to say that his father, Jack, had been placed under hospice care. His next call was to share the sad but ultimately calming news that Jack had died. Jack was 90 years old.

During some wondrous years at Sam Rayburn High School in Pasadena, Texas, Jack became a mentor, guide, shepherd, and eventually a protector for me and the members of my family.

At First Christian Church in Pasadena, Jack served alongside other parents, including my mother, in the oversight and direction of our prodigious youth group. He was glad to behold, while also usually exhausted by, the extraordinary energy which the youth group expended on mission trips in exotic locales like Monterrey, Mexico, and musical tours to intriguing places like Washington, D.C.

We were a going bunch, and Jack went right along, if not always on the bus, then in all the preparations, planning, and prayers that made the trips possible.

And he was there every Sunday evening when our tenacious tribe would gather for devotions, programs on ethics, Bible studies, moments of sharing about the pressures teens experienced at that time, and so much more. I can never recall the events of those days without also recalling Jack and his wife, Maureen. The Vietnam War, race relations and civil rights, the changing roles of women in U.S. culture, the revolution in technology, the cultural explosion in music, and on and on.

Jack was were there one crucial night, a month after I graduated from high school, when my mother's long battle with Hepatitis C came to an end, just like the doctor's prognosis had said it would five years before when her malady had been diagnosed. For as long as I have breath, I will recall the touch of a loving elder named Jack Sullivan, as he gently consoled my two sisters, Mary Beth and Becky, and myself, when we gathered at M.D. Anderson Hospital in Houston to say final farewells to Bennie Lee Smith Hill. Jack's hand was strong and loving when we most needed such strength and love.

After the funeral, and after my uncle and aunt had traveled

from Baltimore to receive my two sisters into their lives and serve as their guardians, Jack and Maureen took me into their home and their hearts for the remainder of the summer until I headed off for college at TCU. A year later, Jack saw me off when I flew out to Los Angeles, to work at All Peoples Christian Church and Community Center.

During the ensuing years, after TCU and graduate school and church positions, we kept in touch, through letters and phone calls, and some incarnational, face-to-face visits. (Jack once made me pose for 30 minutes as he took pictures of me standing in Community's pulpit. I was embarrassed by his attention but humbled by his proud glee. That visit lingers still with strong sentiment even today.)

Each of us gets to where we are because someone, somewhere, someplace was there for us. Jack Sullivan is indubitably in a lofty pantheon of "greats" in my life because he was there for the members of my family and for me and for many others. Jack's life was a vessel of grace, rare and fine and truly salvific.

So I join my gratitude with the many words of thanks expressed by others for Jack and his exemplary life:

- For his abounding love for Maureen that was matched only by his love for his sons, Andy, Darryl, and Tim, and their tribes;
- For his abiding hope in the redemption of every person he ever met;
- For his fidelity to the love of God in Christ which he shared freely without restraint;
- For his gracing patience and steadfast guidance that blessed more people than he ever.

Remembering Denton Roberts

However limited language may be, words are finally what we possess to speak our thanks in honor of those we love. And so I say thanks for Denton Lowell Roberts, Jr., who died on December 12, 2011, in Canon City, Colorado, and whose memorial service was held on February 12, 2012, at All Peoples Christian Church in Los Angeles, California.

I am a "Timothy" of All Peoples and of Denton Roberts. Which means, in church lingo, I'm a person who resolved a call to ministry under Denton's influence at All Peoples. As Paul was to Timothy in the New Testament, Denton has been to me, beginning in 1972 and continuing to this very day.

I met Denton at the front door of the old All Peoples building on the occasion of the thirtieth anniversary of All Peoples' founding. Thereafter Denton would become a friend, pastor, teacher, confidant, mentor, co-author, and a prodding guide and caring gracer along life's path. Denton preached at my ordination, served as best man in Priscilla's and my wedding, and presided at my father's funeral. In turn, I would preside at his mother's funeral, as well as introduce him to Frederick Buechner, Will Campbell, Annie Dillard, Donald Hall, and Johnny Ray Youngblood, along with the wonderments of Kansas City barbecue.

Denton was effective wherever work was set to his hands: in the first church he pastored, Early Chapel in Earlham, Iowa; in a new church started in Livermore, California; praying in jail with William Sloane Coffin and Benjamin Spock; resuscitating a dormant counseling center; steering at the helm of an ITAA committee or special project; offering wisdom before a colloquy of studious Chautauquans in upstate New York; guiding faithful saints at the close of their congregational journey; and proffering his preaching and his pastoral care from the All Peoples pulpit.

Denton was unflagging in his commitments to do what he could in a world racked by pain and rocked by unrest. From the hot days of Selma, to the poverty-scarred streets of South Central Los Angeles, to a nation inebriated on the wine of war, to the hallowed space of Ground Zero in New York, Denton provided leadership and love, presence and prayer, counsel and creativity.

Denton wrote his sermons on Sunday mornings, but he lived with his sermons day by day, week by week, season by season. Denton knew well the Chasidic wisdom: More important than the sermon the rabbi gives, is the sermon the rabbi is.

His devotion to family was surely his greatest gift and his highest accomplishment. As a husband, his vigilant care for Jerry as she dealt with a terminal disease remains an example for all husbands to follow. His loving nurture of his sons Dane and Courtney was simply superb. And his puckish delight in his grandchildren, Wilson, Zoey, Jamie, and Zach, increased with his every breath, as he witnessed the blossoming of his most recent legacy.

While there was part of Denton that clung to Dylan Thomas' charge not to "go gentle into that good night," he became increasingly comfortable with his status as "a lion in winter."

Denton truly lived out the titles of his books. He had his lumps and bumps. But he was able and equal. He found purpose and power. He lived as a healer. He empowered congregations and organizations.

Denton was a theoretician, but he did not live theoretically. He met others with clear-minded insights, an unfettered intuition that bordered on genius, and a deeply compassionate heart. He was the least threatened human being I ever met, and I cannot imagine meeting his match in the future.

Not only was Denton all those attributes and qualities, he is those same attributes and qualities, as he lives on in those who wear his genes, Dane and Cort and their loving extended family, and in all of his friends and collaborators. This is what the truth of faith teaches us: not only *was*, but *is*. And now as a child of God enjoying eternal peace within God's loving embrace, Denton still is. As it is with Denton Lowell Roberts, Jr., let it be so with all of us, today and forever.

Remembering Dale Eldred

Although Dale Eldred's design fulfilled Frank Lloyd Wright's 1940 vision for Community's Steeple of Light, Dale never got to see it come into being. As well as an internationally acclaimed sculptor, Dale was chair of the Sculpture Department at the Kansas City Art Institute for 33 years. During his brief 59 years he accomplished herculean tasks and mammoth projects.

Described once as a proponent of romantic gigantism, he became best known for large-scale sculptures that included natural and generated light. He created numerous works of art in Kansas City and around the world. He inspired and launched hundreds of art students in their luminous careers. But he never was afforded the earthly pleasure of standing with family and friends to behold the Steeple of Light at the corner of 46th and Main.

In the summer of 1993, Dale and the rest of Kansas City were worried about the rising of the Missouri River due to the 500-year flood affecting the heartland. On July 26, 1993, with the assistance of his artistic crew, Dale was moving equipment in his two-story West Bottoms studio in preparation for possible flooding. On the studio's second floor, Dale, who rarely ever forgot where his feet were, forgot that a grate had been set aside and tripped and fell through the opening to the ground floor below. His death was devastating to family and friends, to Kansas City, and to the artistic community here and around the world. Those who gathered for the memorial service celebrating his life mourned his death and blessed his legacy.

Dale's art continues to bless people and places around the world: in the hinterlands of Turkey; in the Nashville airport; in downtown Kansas City, Kansas; along a North Carolina causeway; in the Tulsa Convention Center; in an Illinois shopping center; at a Des Moines art center; at the Minneapolis Institute for the Arts; at a Denver education center; in a Fort Lauderdale library; on college campuses in Missouri, Kansas, Michigan, Ohio, Oregon, Utah, and Arizona; and in numerous personal art collections around the world.

Dale's long, grand romance with light was an ultimate testimony to his love of beauty. For light has a twin identity: first, light illumines all things, and without it nothing is illuminated; second, the illumination of light becomes a marvelous, alluring enchantment in and of itself. As a perpetual kindergartner on his way to the perpetual first day of school, Dale delighted in light's capacity to empower him in a grand, perpetual game of "Show and Tell." Or as Dale might have said: light shows great beauty and it tells great truth.

To me, more important than his prodigious talent, more crucial than his unique gifts, more telling than his insatiable curiosity, more impressive than his powerful personality, and more searing than the piercing glint of his keen vision, this is first and foremost: Dale Eldred was a friend, rare and fine and precious.

Let us be thankful that we are the stewards of one of Dale's most visible and accessible sculptures, the Steeple of Light, made possible by his design and by the artistic execution of Roberta Lord, his partner in all things. More importantly, let us be thankful for Dale Eldred himself, who abides in loving memory as friend, teacher, colleague, brother, uncle, father, husband, partner, child of God, brother of the light, progeny of the Eternal.

Remembering Forrest Church

On September 24, 2009, Forrest Church, beloved husband, father, brother, son, friend, and Minister of Public Theology and former Senior Minister of All Souls Unitarian Church in New York City for nearly thirty years, died in peace, his life fully extended, his love now embracing eternity.

I met Forrest in the aftermath of 9/11. We made a connection in New York City while Priscilla and I were enjoying the East Coast leg of my sabbatical. How we actually came to meet in his office at the corner of Lexington Ave. and 80th St. was a mystery to us both, through a happenstance e-mail, as best we could figure. Regardless of the manner of our meeting, his gracious hospitality and kindnesses were, as they always would be, consistent and enduring, the stuff of which dear friendships is made. I was glad to offer a poetic piece to a book he was putting together then (*Restoring Faith: America's Religious Leaders Answer Terror with Hope*). I was also glad when he began making stops at Community on his book tours, as he read from *Freedom from Fear*, *The American Creed*, and, two years ago, *So Help Me God: The Founding Fathers and the First Great Battle Over Church and State*. But an even greater grace was the sheer joy one could share with Forrest, talking baseball, politics, theology, family dynamics, books, history, barbecue, Idaho lore, New York City wonders, and the blessedness of the pastoral life.

In addition to pastoring the membership of All Souls, Forrest was the author or editor of 25 books. In November, Beacon Press will publish his last book, *The Cathedral of the World: a Universalist Theology*. He also served in leadership capacities throughout New York City, and offered commentary for CNN, ABC, NBC, and CBS news, as well as for National Public Radio.

Forrest's family will gratefully recall how his love and care were persistently, passionately present. History will show him to have been an extraordinary clergyman, leading the once quiescent All Souls Unitarian Church in New York City to become the flagship congregation of the Unitarian Universalists in the United States. All Souls congregants will surely witness how the love they shared with their pastor was exemplary and life-changing, the way all ministers hope relationships to be. Friends will attest that his openheartedness was rare, fine, and a blessed source of encouragement.

It is likely that Forrest's most lasting legacy will turn out to be the manner in which he faced death, after learning that he had esophageal cancer in 2006. Joyful to the point of buoyancy, Forrest's posture of gratitude for daily grace afforded him enough time to complete three more books. And good for all his thankful readers, each tome set forth a distinct aspect of his public life: his conclusive historian's assessment (*So Help Me God*), his overarching pastoral perspective (*Love and Death*), and his final theological statement (*The Cathedral of the World*).

In honor of Forrest's life and in celebration of his amazing graciousness in the midst of life and death, I offer here a poem which was a gift at the occasion of his 60th birthday celebration last year.

In the World's Cathedral
(for Forrest Church)

And so we gathered, and so he made it,
as he said he could, as we knew
he would, to the hallmark birthday,
and all because of the radiance,
ablaze in his eyes,
which he borrowed fully
from the light, always slanting,
shimmering, with audacious freedom,
in the world's cathedral.

As son, husband, father,
prophet, poet, priest,
all these, and friend, too, he said
what he had been saying
all along, the one thing
that always wins, always lasts:
our tears in another's eyes,
flowing from the source
that conquers every fear.

We told him good joy,

we returned to him what he had given
freely, a glad, grateful peace,
which he grants, even now,
to those here and to those coming
in a new legacy, and this too:
the best courage, the best oration,
the best oblation is love. Love. Love,
his for us all and ours for him, forever

Nelson Mandela, Thank You

When the news of Nelson Mandela's death was transmitted around the world last week, my immediate response was to say out loud: "Nelson Mandela, thank you for your hope-saturated courage and unfailing love for humanity. The light of your indomitable spirit has not gone out." I said it again while watching the broadcast of his memorial service. I said it both as a hope and a conviction, a stone-serious testimony. It's amazing to realize how much Nelson Mandela's unflagging courage and tenacity have impacted so many.

Always Mandela was a paragon of indefatigable strength, prior to, during, and especially after his long years of imprisonment. Oh, how he then infused peace into each encounter, offering the cool waters of forgiveness and reconciliation from a deep well of good will.

Mandela was and will remain in my mind a giant of gentleness, a defender of the defenseless, a faithful exemplar of reconciliation when reconciliation seemed futile. Vilified as a communist, condemned as a terrorist, the conscience of a movement, the Father of a nation, a troubler of those waters that desperately needed troubling, a stellar exemplar of healing forgiveness, not only for his country but for the world.

I can hardly remember a time in my adult life when Nelson Mandela wasn't a powerful, hovering force for transformation in the world and an inspirational force in the lives of innumerable admirers. His marvelous journey and his magisterial measure of morality unfolded before our very lives, year after year.

During my first year of divinity school in Nashville, Tennessee, I heard Dennis Brutus, a visiting scholar, poet, and sports activist from South Africa, tell how he had occupied a prison cell next to Nelson Mandela's on Robben Island, where Mandela spent 18 of his 27 years of incarceration. Hearing Brutus' stories prompted my first public witness involvement, as I joined my voice with others to protest South Africa's dreaded apartheid system of racial discrimination.

Several years later, during a study leave in the summer of 1988, I ventured on a two-and-a-half week tour of South Africa's exquisitely beautiful land, prior to Mandela's release from prison. One could sense his lingering aura of fierce faith and intense hopefulness, as he came up in conversations again and again.

A couple of years later, while visiting Senator Dole's and Senator Bond's offices in Washington, D.C., in an effort to urge U.S. disengagement from South Africa and its apartheid policies, I had an awareness of Mandela's overarching influence in many such citizen-motivated efforts.

And I will never forget the day of his ultimate release from prison, on Sunday, February 11, 1990, when Scott Stuart greeted me at Community's Main Street door after worship with a joyful exclamation, "He's out! He's free! Mandela's finally been released!"

Then there was Mr. Mandela's democratic election as the first black President of South Africa in 1994, and the creation of the Truth and Reconciliation Commission, chaired by his friend Archbishop Desmond Tutu, in 1995. And then came the South African Constitution, which he had a significant hand in framing, and his daring decision not to seek a second term.

In sacred defiance, Nelson Mandela led in the dismantling of apartheid's diabolical walls of division. In his determined fidelity to democracy, he constructed a pathway toward authentic freedom, a blessed right which all humanity deserves. And he did it, all the while, by allowing the peace of God to dwell in him and to shape his relationships.

Thank you, Nelson Mandela! And thanks be to God for the privilege of living during a time in history when such a man, such a great soul, such a leader was ours to behold.

Giving Thanks for Howard Thurman

November 18th is the 115th anniversary of Howard Thurman's birth. I remain eternally grateful to God that my mentor and friend Kelly Miller Smith introduced Howard Thurman to me during my years in Nashville, Tennessee. Rarely has the religious scene in America seen in one person such a combination of pastoral sensitivity to persons, respect for a wide range of spiritual disciplines, and prophetic insight into remedies for social injustice.

Thurman was a person of firsts. In 1936, he was part of the first African-American entourage to visit Mohandas Gandhi in India and thereafter to bring Gandhi's strategic ethic of nonviolence to the U.S. In 1944, in San Francisco, Thurman was a founding pastor of The Church for the Fellowship of All Peoples, the first intentionally interracial, interdenominational church in the U.S. In 1953, he was the first African-American to become Dean of the Marsh Chapel at Boston University. During the height of his powers, *Life* magazine esteemed him as one of the 12 greatest preachers of the 20th century.

Twice I've been graced to experience profound encounters with Thurman's legacy: (1) the occasion to preach from his former pulpit in San Francisco, and (2) the discovery of his first book, *The Greatest of These*, tucked neatly away on the shelves of the Pendle Hill Retreat Center library near Philadelphia. In both cases Thurman's powerful presence was nearly palpable. Since those experiences, I've grown increasingly indebted to Thurman for his enduring impact on religionists in America and around the globe.

Always in the forefront of Thurman's thought and work was his unwavering commitment to "the search for common ground." His overall vision was "a friendly world underneath friendly skies." His autobiography, *With Head and Heart*, ought to be required reading for every seminary student.

How we need Thurman's influence these days! As we pass by Thurman's birthday anniversary in advance of our Thanksgiving holiday observance, I invite you to join me in saying "Thanks be to God" for Howard Thurman.

Introduction and Tribute for Fred Craddock- July 11, 2011

Disciples Divinity House, Vanderbilt Divinity School Luncheon, at the time of the 2011 General Assembly o the Christian Church (Disciples of Christ), Nashville, Tennessee

Other than being the premier homiletician leading in the reclamation and renewal of the discipline and practice of preaching for the church in North America at the end of the 20th century and into the 21st century; and

Other than being the most acclaimed Disciple preacher of the last 50 years; and

Other than being one of the most faithful of Disciples — faithful to the witness of scripture, faithful to his calling, faithful to ecclesia, faithful to the academy, faithful to Nettie and to family and to Cherry Log and to friends and to God;

Other than all of what others have already said so well, how does one introduce a man who is known far and wide by the sheer, gentle, yet persuasive force of his first name, "Fred"?

Well, let us consider, in a truly inductive manner:

1 – PLACE

Maybe it is because of what we have learned from Fred about *place* that we gather to honor him. Fred has taught us the value of place, the specifics of place and the nuances of place. He has witnessed in his own life as to the importance of place, in that he was dedicated, baptized, ordained, and married in one particular place, Central Avenue Christian Church in Humboldt, Tennessee. Even if you've never crossed the city limits in a vehicle, Fred has taken you there. Because of what Fred has taught us, we know that *that* place and all of the places we all of us value are so very essentially, crucially important.

2 – PLACEMENT

Maybe we gather in this honoring moment because of how Fred has reminded us of the significance of placement, how we place ourselves at the disposal of others for service and fellowship,

how we place our words as best we can in the service of the
gospel and its love-endearing, hate-shattering powers.

It could be that. But maybe not.

3 – PEOPLE
Perhaps we're gathered here because of the people Fred has
reminded us of, some we knew about and some we never would
have known without his illumination of their lives.
- Hermann Diem
- Soren Kierkegaard
- Frederick W. Robertson
- Albert Schweitzer
- Ben Hooper

Because of how Fred illumined their lives for us, we have been
emboldened to pay better attention to the people with whom we
share life and love and faith.

One thing I am almost 100% sure of is this:

4 – THE POWER OF A REMEMBERED PHRASE
I believe we are gathered here to pay tribute to Fred, because of
the power of a remembered phrase or a story or an
admonishment or a challenge or an encouragement. You
remember them, don't you, those phrases, those beautiful,
arresting flourishes? We've heard them when Fred was giving a
seminary presentation, or fulfilling a lectureship, or offering his
wise advice, or when he was preaching in our churches or at a
General Assembly. You remember those daring theological
declarations, like:

"Anticipation is the key. Phone ahead before you make a
pastoral visit. Anticipation of a visit is half of the pleasure for
those who receive the pastor into their homes."

"Did you bring 'Doxology' with you?"

"When your faith fades and grows dim, let your congregation
believe for you until your faith returns."

"Gracious God, we are grateful for a way of life and work that is more important than how we feel about it on any given day."

"If you're tired, go to bed, and, later, make an appointment with God..."

The cavernous distance between "the sky of our intentions and the earth of our performance..."

"... nine-pound sparrow..."

"The final work of grace in the human heart is to make us grateful."

Because of these memorable phrases — and so many others, too numerous to count — Fred has inspired us all to know just how powerful preaching and teaching and faith can be, and to never take those tasks glibly or without proper prayer and preparation.

CONCLUSION – Story - "SHE WANTS SOME NAMES."
In a story Fred tells — a story which, for lack of a title, goes by the legendary title "She Wants Some Names"[1] – Fred once encountered, in a church in Oklahoma, a woman who shocked him by saying she was quitting the choir (and ostensibly the congregation). When Fred pressed her about why, she said no one cared for her. When he asked her what it would take for the church to show her they cared, she said "Take me seriously." She wanted some names of folks who took her seriously and cared for her.

If that woman, or someone like her, were here today, I would say, on behalf of us all, "You want some names? I know someone who will take you seriously, someone who will care for you deeply, as he had for countless students, colleagues, church members and friends. I know someone. You want his name? His name is Fred Craddock. I know he cares."

Fred, on behalf of the Disciples Divinity House of Vanderbilt

---

[1] See Fred. B. Craddock, *Craddock Stories*, edited by Mike Graves and Richard F. Ward (St. Louis: Chalice Press, 2001), pp. 58-60.

Divinity School, we offer you our profoundest "Thanks."

—Bob Hill

A Nobel Prize for Wendell Berry

I've heard that Wendell Berry won't let any friends or associates form a campaign committee to get him nominated and, hopefully, chosen as a recipient for a Nobel Prize. That's a shame on two accounts. It's a shame that such a campaign committee should be necessary for such an award. And it's a shame, if such a committee really is a necessity, that Berry won't let it be formed.

I can think of few writers in American letters as esteemed as Berry is. Author of 14 books of fiction (novels and short stories), 29 books of nonfiction (essays, criticism, social commentary, biography), 26 substantive introductions, prefaces, forewords, or afterwords (for books by others), and 26 volumes of poetry (which is, in my estimation, his strongest genre), Wendell Berry, 77 years old, has provided galvanizing inspiration and wise guidance throughout his writing life.

At the same time, for most of his years as an inscriber of words, he has done so as a horse-drawn-plough farmer and an unwavering advocate for healing stewardship of the earth. And he has written and ploughed and advocated as a clear-eyed, deep-hearted person of faith. The number of assessments and scholarly works about his place and value as a commentator and source of inspiration is legion.

No doubt many of Community's members and friends can recollect the numerous references I've made to Berry in sermons. And some may even have grown tired of my recommending his Sabbath poems collection, *A Timbered Choir*, as a devotional masterpiece deserving of everyone's attention.

I'll make a quick deal, right now, however. I'll tone down my recommendations when Wendell Berry is in either Stockholm or Oslo receiving a Nobel Prize. It's difficult to anticipate whether he deserves it more for literature or for peace. His contributions to both have been profound and prodigious.

Famous Babies

I recently told my friend Seymour about all the babies being born among Community families these days, some even slated for their first earthly performance this month.

"Famous babies are born in January," Seymour opined. Then Seymour provided evidence, saying, "Yes, it's true. Did you know that Abraham Joshua Heschel, Albert Schweitzer, Martin Luther King, Jr., Henri Nouwen, Rufus Jones, Mahalia Jackson, and Thomas Merton were all born in the month of January?"

I admitted that I didn't. But then I got to thinking about the wonderful lives Community's January children will live, how famous they will become.

Which also got me to thinking about the Community babies that were born this past fall and before, and those that are going to be born in coming months, and all the babies that will be born far into the future.

Which then prompted me to conclude that Seymour is 8.33% right. Famous babies are born in January. But they're also born in February, March, April, May, June, July, August, September, October, November, and December.

And we don't have to wait until they're grown up to see what they'll do to become famous. Babies are already famous. Just ask a mother of a newborn. Or a father. Or a grandmother. Or a grandfather. Or an aunt. Or an uncle. Just ask a church.

Overcoming Great Odds

Somehow life's most lavish accolades are reserved for the truly great, who usually have overcome great odds (of poverty, disinterest, or public neglect) and lived a life of devotion to premier principles, service for others, and supplication to a purpose and a power higher than their own ego or vanity. Consider:

Mohandas K. Gandhi died owning less than ten material items, valued in pennies. But he led the liberation of one of the world's largest nations.

Mahalia Jackson was born in extreme poverty to unwed parents, with a voice that defied training, categorization, and, in the beginning, much recognition. Yet, through her fidelity to the art of gospel songs, she provided the church and the world a whole new way of praising God, singing before presidents and kings and queens and wholly inspired congregations.

Howard Thurman was born in extremely challenging circumstances, amidst the devastating oppression of a deeply segregated Florida. But he is now being recalled as one of America's premier Christian mystics and most profound theologians.

Agnes Gonxha Bojaxhiu came from the nearly negligible town of Skopje, Albania, never married, worked among the destitute and the downtrodden, issued very few noteworthy publications, owned almost nothing. Yet, both Protestants and Catholics called her Mother Teresa.

His mother's name was Effy, and she brought him as a child to their church, Community, at Linwood and Forest (Community's location prior to 1939). He struggled with childhood ailments, one of which kept him on his back for a year. He strove mightily in sales, but he never could quite get what was duly coming to him. So he started up his own enterprise. He was successful beyond his wildest dreams. But the greatest pleasure Ewing Kauffman took in life, and the sweetest satisfactions he garnered from his business, were the capacity to give away millions of dollars so that Kansas Citians could enjoy Royals baseball and the establishment of the Kauffman Foundation legacy.

Yes, this week the truth of Reba Fichthorn's poem seers its impression into heart and mind:

> My life shall touch a dozen lives before this day is done.
> Leave countless marks for good or ill ere sets the evening sun.
> This is my wish I always wish, the prayer I always pray:
> Lord, may my life help other lives it touches by the way.

The Greatness of Gary Straub

From a porch on the east side of the main lodge at the
Loretto House in Nyrynx, Kentucky, to a fog-shrouded retreat
center by Puget Sound, to the desk where he meets his daily
obligation of prayer and writing and brooding over the present
prospects and future fulfillment of the gospel in the 21st century,
Gary Straub has been and is at the heart of the Bethany Project
and the Bethany Fellows.

Gary has taught and inspired in us so much — so much
more than this evening or any evening would allow us to
describe. We have the sentiments but not the time to give
account of all that he has meant to so many people and all he has
meant to each of us.

So this will be painfully, awkwardly, brutally, but
necessarily brief.

Greatness is the word I would use to describe my estimation
of Gary Straub. Greatness.

Not greatness in the sense of great preaching, though he is a
great preacher, full of the Word and effulgent with poetic
eloquence to proclaim that Word.

Nor do I mean greatness in the sense of being an exemplary
spiritual guide on the path of faith, an identity he has fulfilled
beautifully for thousands of people — as a pastor, as a colleague,
as a spiritual director, as a team member, as a friend.

Nor do I mean greatness in the sense of being an encourager,
although he has been and done that in spades. There are few if
any in my experience who have been as consistent and as
enduring in their encouragement as Gary Straub. He is a
Barnabas of the first rank to so many lives, including my own.

Nor do I mean greatness in the sense of immersing himself
in the great blessings of prayer, which is his chief *métier*. There is
no way to measure how many times Gary has prayed for the
Bethany Fellows, for each of us, and for the growth and vitality
of the Church we abide in and the congregations we serve. But
we know he has prayed for us — individually and collectively,
over long stretches of time and across the miles. Younger pastors
have felt it in the resilient rebounding of their spirits after a
tough time. They have known it in the refreshment of their

congregations during moments of transition and renewal. We all have been touched by it in occasions of epiphany, as we've read a sacred text or written a sermon or counseled a sojourner or searched for mercy in the valley of the shadow or bowed in prayer before the God of our lives.

No, I mean greatness in another, more profound sense. Gary Straub has been, and is, and will remain great because he evokes, elicits, prods and promotes greatness in others. This is the true measure, I believe, of whether or not a person is deserving of the moniker of being "great." One who draws out the greatness of those around him, who prompts the expression of greatness in his friends' lives, who yearns and prays and aches and hopes for greatness to be a reality for the gospel's sake in the lives of the Bethany Fellows — this is Gary Straub.

But sometimes, there isn't greatness enough in us to evoke or elicit, to prod or promote. Whether because of circumstance or predicament or life situation, the experience and expression of greatness isn't possible for us. Then Gary shifts gears and draws out of others their best selves, draws out of us our best selves. And when that happens, it's like a rainbow after a deluge, like a new sprout of life coming forth from a stump long thought dead and gone, like a stone rolled away and an Easter dawning. And Gary has done that for all of us well.

But sometimes, there isn't even enough of our best selves to evoke or elicit, to prod or promote. Sometimes we've "been down so long it looks like up to us." Sometimes we feel "like a motherless child." Sometimes the heartaches have been so hurtful, the confusions so crass, and the dilemmas so daunting that there is no greatness or best-ness that can be found. Then Gary proffers perhaps his most profound gift, the invitation for folks to be themselves as children of God, to be ourselves, to be yourself, to simply *be* with as much authenticity as we can muster, and to know that such authenticity is blessed not only by his admiring esteem but by God's holy love.

This is what I believe Gary means, at least in part, for the endeavor known as Bethany, and what he means to us in the leadership circle, and what he means to me – one who draws out of others their greatness, and if not their greatness, then their best selves, and if not their best selves, then their authentic lives in full wonderment, upheld by God's grace.

This is what makes Gary great.

We've seen this quality before, and we recognize it for what it is. Gary is great in the way Christ was great in his relationships with his first followers, the way Christ's spirit has been great down through the ages, the way Christ's empowering presence is great among us now. Gary's Christ-like greatness causes us now to rise and call him blessed.

TRUE TREASURES

Treasure

Signs and symbols of encouragement, those special windows on the numinous, are everywhere, really, if we will but have eyes and ears and hearts and minds and souls open and prepared to take them all in. They can even surprise us in the most unlikely of places, like a plane ride.

On an airplane several years ago, I listened with uncharacteristic attention to the flight attendant as she instructed us passengers with the requisite pantomime motions about the appropriate procedures for exiting the plan in the event of a premature downing and subsequent safe landing. In contrast to most flight instructions, the guidance, this time, was powerfully, uncharacteristically different.

The attendant instructing us had a lapel pin with some wings on it and the word "Treasure" clearly imprinted on top of it. "Treasure?" What kind of treasure, I wondered. Was this a new one-word branding — a synopsis of the airline's new mission statement? ("We treasure the opportunity to serve you with a treasure trip aboard one of our airborne treasures.") Or was there a different explanation? Could it be a name she had given herself, breaking the bounds of family and tribe, expressing her own preference, her own self-naming, self-creating? Or could it be, I wondered further, a family name, her mother's maiden name, given to her to carry on a memory of matrilineal connections? Perhaps she was the late-flowering child of some left-over hippies who wanted to give her a name to live into? (A couple I met once named their late-surprise son Funn because they wanted him to have as much fun in his life as they had had in theirs.)

Whatever its origins, the word itself, "Treasure," was a rare and fine gift, just the word I needed, to see, to behold, to hear, to receive as my current marching orders for the living of my days, at least at that time.

When the epiphany was granted, however, it was, at first, a challenge to figure out if the word was a verb or a noun. The answer that came? Yes.

Treasure, as a verb, yes, to hold dear, to be fond of, to be so glad in the presence of that which you cherish and those whom you esteem. Treasure, hold close and dear those aspects of your life that are far more precious than any material thing. Treasure a seed falling to the ground in October's swirling air. Treasure the taste of an apple picked straight from a tree. Treasure the crinkle-crackle of the pages of a Bible, particularly the Psalms, especially during difficult, cacophonous times. Treasure. Yes, a verb.

But treasure, too, as a noun. Treasure, as in something highly prized for beauty or perfection, or both. Treasure, as in gift, as in valuable above almost all other valuables we might possess. Treasure, as in some thing or some one appreciated above nearly all others. Treasure, as in treasure chest, as in the commodity for which we might offer some of our treasury to procure, as in a famed island where a cache of gold doubloons awaits eager and crafty hunters. Yes, treasure as noun. Yes.

Both as verb and as a noun, the word "treasure," as the philosopher Paul Ricoeur would quickly remind us, had an autonomy of its own on that airplane. It had a shape and an impact and a usage far beyond its purposes on the attendant's lapel pin. For to treasure is a fundamental purpose for human life. Beyond the ability to wiggle opposable thumbs, maybe our uniqueness as a species really has to do with our capacity to treasure the treasures that have been proffered into our hands.

When I asked the attendant the meaning of the word on her lapel pin, she said it was her given name. How many other passengers on our flight or on previous flights had taken comfort in this angelic message on the pristine uniform blouse of this cherubic steward, I don't know. How many others had encountered her parable-of-a-name, one will never know.

I fantasized about calling up her parents, or better, choosing a piece of thick stationery and writing a note, a paean of praise and unabashed gratitude for the saving wisdom that possessed them to hang such a moniker on her and have her gladly live it out, embody it, in front of God and everybody everywhere she happened to go.

Treasure might have been the name the proud and pleased parents gave to a daughter who was truly their actual treasure, somewhere way over a rainbow of their hopes and dreams. She and her name are surely a treasure to me, even now, as I remember that plane ride and that lapel pin ten years later.

The Challenge (and Centrality) of Superlatives

"Longest Drive," "Closest Relative," "Tallest Building," "Deepest Canyon," "Highest Salary," "Best Street Tacos," "Thinnest Bible," "Hottest Summer," "Coldest Winter," "Smallest Seed," "Biggest Watermelon"... of course, such a list could go on and on. We know the rationale and impetus behind the *Guinness Book of World Records*: we mark our existence constantly by superlatives.

Driving through Missouri and Kansas alone can teach you this salient truth, as you behold signs and indicators for world's largest prairie dog, or world's largest ball of twine, or the best frozen custard west of the Mississippi. And you can't really blame the human family for being so inclined.

Now, expressing superlatives can get in the way of living life as it is given. If we make idols of what we (and others) take to be "the best," "the finest," or "the greatest," we may miss the enchantments of daily gifts, which truly are best, finest, or greatest, even while they are masquerading as mundane. Some cultural observers might critique the U.S. as being obsessed about superlatives.

Still, superlatives are central and important for the human prospect. Even in congregations we have this motivating impulse. Is there a body of believers anywhere that doesn't think about itself, at least from time to time, as the "best" or "most" in some kind of category — "the warmest welcome," "the most caring fellowship," "the best singing," "the most loving servants?"

Far from being instances of braggadocio or brazenness, such superlative descriptions are the responses of the faithful who have been inspired by a story that is itself saturated with superlatives of size and scope.

In humility and hope, as we see a world so much in need of the gospel's truth and power, allow me to muse on our collective penchant for "best" and "most" with the following question: Is there any other way?

What's Your Undertone?

As much as I admire Frederick W. Robertson, the great 19th century divine (esteemed by some as the greatest preacher in the English tongue), I was caught off-guard when I leaned about one of his basic tenets of faith. I was dismayed to read about what I would call Robertson's regrettable understanding of human experience: "The deep undertone of the world is sadness."

I am sure that there are countless people who would agree with the "Bright Light of Brighton," particularly since there are so many occasions for sadness throughout the world and in our own lives. But to say that the world's fundamental undertone is sadness seems to me to be a mistaking of the human experience as a whole and a misinterpretation of the Biblical witness.

The undertones of the world are many and varied. Sorrow, to be sure, is an undertone in Oklahoma and elsewhere where tornadoes have wreaked such havoc and horror. But relief and satisfaction and gladness and celebration are also undertones in every commencement exercise going on at colleges and high schools these days.

Beauty seems to be one of the premier undertones of our world, with spring freshly sprung (finally!) and the greening of Kansas City everywhere on display.

Adventure, excitement, and fun are going to be the undertones of Community's forthcoming Vacation Bible School.

Growth and grace will surely be the abiding undertones of our Youth Mission Trip later on this summer.

Appreciation and remembrance will be among the undertones for people visiting cemeteries and grave sites this coming Memorial Day weekend. But so will reunion, affirmation, and love for friends and families gathering for picnics, fireworks, and the essential sacrament of sharing stories.

There are undertones in all families of faith as well, including at Community. An important question for all congregations is this: Which undertones prevail among us, undertones of faith, hope, and love, or undertones of perplexity, despair, and wandering?

May the predominant undertones at Community remain the former sorts!

Some Contemporary Beatitudes

The Beatitudes of Jesus are among the strongest challenges for human conduct and religious life ever inscribed. While they can never be improved upon, pondering new ways of being blessed can stimulate our faith. Thus, the following, a contemporized list of beatitudes for consideration:

- Blessed are you when you grow sick and tired of being sick and tired, for you will know where your real strength comes from.
- Blessed are you when, in the face of tragedy and horror, you are reduced to mute tears, for then you will know the eloquence of God's embrace and the profundity of God's presence.
- Blessed are you when you've been rejected, dejected, and perhaps even ejected from a relationship, an association, or a job — because of a stance you have taken — for then you will know the gift of integrity and courage.
- Blessed are you when your money runs out, for then you will discover true wealth.
- Blessed are you when you finally "fess up" to not knowing how to pray, for then you will have opened the door to truly listening for God's voice.
- Blessed are you when you participate in lifesaving strategies like Heifer International's "Passing on the Gift," for then, one day, you will see the whole world fed and fit.
- Blessed are you when you are in the midst of a medical crisis, for then you will have begun a journey into true patience, authentic humility, and blatant, unadorned, stupefying gratitude.

Whataburger Thanksgiving

One Thanksgiving season, down in Brownsville, Texas, in the verdant environs of the Rio Grande Valley, the site of my childhood years, our family, headed by our single mother, Bennie Lee Smith Hill, along with the chirpy contributions of her three young children, including my younger sisters, Mary Beth and Becky, and me, made a revolutionary decision about what we were going to have for Thanksgiving dinner.

Our mother, in a fit of either sheer genius or stupefied exasperation, threw it open to our discretion as to what we would have as our delectable fare on that forthcoming Thanksgiving day.

"Well," she said — and we always knew it was either trouble or adventure when she began a sentence with that onerous sounding "Well..." — "what would you like to have for Thanksgiving dinner? You get to pick." We couldn't believe our ears! Whatever we wanted, whatever we decided, that's what it would be!

Together and individually, my sisters and I ruminated about our choice and what she actually had in mind. Maybe she wanted us to just pick mashed potatoes or our grandmother Mammy's special recipe for cornbread dressing. Or maybe we'd side with Mary Beth, who always seemed to end up with a red tongue by the conclusion of Thanksgiving Day because she had eaten so much cranberry jelly. Or maybe we would simply bypass the turkey and go for what we truly enjoyed, chicken.

Later on we would wonder if our mother was simply trying to avoid the swamping sense of fatigue that can sometimes overcome one's heart and mind and body and soul at Thanksgiving time.

Whatever the reason, she cut us a square deal: we could pick what we were going to eat, and that would be the decision. We made her repeat it, a couple of times, to make sure we had heard right. And when we had secured the official and final confirmation, we exclaimed, almost all at once, almost in one voice: "WHATABURGER!"

Now Whataburger is a franchised chain of hamburger joints down in Texas, in other parts of the Southwest, and in the tropical climes of the South. We didn't know that then, but we'd learn it later. All we knew was that the iconic A-frame, white-and-orange corrugated tin Whataburger buildings were the absolute best places on the face of the earth to eat. You ate a Whataburger burger, and you said immediately, just like their ads said you'd say, "WHATABURGER!" We loved to say that phrase, and we loved to eat those burgers, and that was our choice.

Our mother kept her word, and we did indeed and in fact eat our Whataburger burgers at the glorious Whataburger on Boca Chica Boulevard on Thanksgiving Day that year. There was something marvelous and mysterious and altogether totally in keeping with the American spirit of Thanksgiving in that moment. As we ate our burgers in the delicious freedom of having our own choice, we had done our mother a great favor, I believe. She was all smiles in the face of all of our smiles. She had made her boisterous children blissfully happy. And she had salvaged so much of the family budget because the burgers were on sale, three for one, just for that Thanksgiving Day! Now the American spirit was not merely in the cheapness of the meal but more in the grace of having saved each other with the freedom of a choice and the satisfying sufficiency of sharing what there was to share.

Our mother had saved us from all that we had dreaded to encounter at the traditional family Thanksgiving gathering — a great-aunt's venerated yet, to us three children, inedible picnic pickles, a distant second cousin's mincemeat pie which no amount of whipped cream could atone for, and our childlike embarrassment over the absence of our father. And she had saved us for an encounter with sheer joy and gladness and satisfaction.

And our mother, struggling as she was with so much pressure and a sense of something, I am sure, that, to her, smelled and tasted like helplessness, was saved by the delight in our eyes, our unmitigated glee at being able to eat at Whataburger!

In this manner our family came to know what we all know about this sacred season, namely, "You don't necessarily have to have a turkey to have Thanksgiving." And, in an intimately real way, we also came to know one of the foundational touchstones of our nation's most inclusive holiday: Thanksgiving is really about being saved — saved from degradation, shame, and souladdling drudgery. And being saved for the blessing of togetherness and the savoring of joyful fullness.

Down through the years, on the way to one Thanksgiving dinner or another, I've passed by any number of fast-food joints. Each time I've offered up a blessing of gladness for the people there, however they came to their places at those tables. Who knows? The tight little bunches of two or three or four, sheltered under those fluorescent lights, might be exercising their own saving choices.

Also, down through the years, after arriving at the appointed Thanksgiving celebration sites, I have enjoyed many fine Thanksgiving dinners with varying menus and a sacred host of beautiful friends and family members. But whenever I am finished and push away from the table, I go back in my memory to Boca Chica Boulevard, and say a phrase, as I am sure my sisters say as well, in honor of our mother and in remembrance of a time and a moment in which we were saved, if not for eternity, then at least for a day. I say it simply, quietly, as a prayer of thanks and exultant joy. I say ... "WHATABURGER!"

Trip to Angola

Last week I was a guest presenter in a unique conference at the Louisiana State Penitentiary in Angola. Community's own Carol McAdoo has a special connection with the renowned hospice program there, and she had worked closely with the folks at Angola, particularly legendary (and controversial) Warden Burl Cain, and Jamey Boudreaux, who heads up the Louisiana & Mississippi Hospice Care and Palliative Care Organization, to put together a four-day training conference for inmate volunteers from Angola and five other prisons within Louisiana's corrections department.

It was Carol who prompted Community's recent and immensely successful hosting of Lori Waslchuk's *Grace Before Dying* photographs which highlighted the Angola hospice program. In connection with that exhibit and Ms. Waselchuk's presence with us, Myra Christopher and the Center for Practical Bioethics hosted the Kansas City premier of the movie *Serving Life*, also about the Angola hospice program. And it was this same hospice program at Angola that, last year, welcomed Rev. Melissa St. Clair, Rev. Michelle Harris-Gloyer, Rev. Megan Ammann, Rev. Ryan Motter, Rev. Steve Mason, and nine other clergy residents from other Transition into Ministry programs like Community's in an immersion experience, also coordinated by Carol and Jamey.

Now I have seen the genesis of Carol's passionate work and know why she is esteemed as one of the premier consultants in the U.S. in the area of aging and dying in prisons. I was honored to be part of the occasion, along with fellow Kansas Citians John Shuster, Patricia Kane and Linda Redford, as well as Carol. But I was humbled as I proffered my two presentations, "Spirituality and Death" and "Dealing with Death: Straight Up, No Chaser."

Though I was invited to Angola to teach and share, it was the inmate volunteers who taught me significant insights about life and death and redemption. As I beheld the insignia on the Angola hospice worker T-shirts ("Helping Others Share their Pain Inside Correctional Environment"), I saw anew the core truths of Christ's way:

- redemption is possible for all of humanity no matter our

circumstance or predicament;

- we are inextricably bound together in life by common essentials — food, shelter, and the need for compassionate validation;
- at the end of life, comfort and care and sympathetic conversation are rich graces which every one of us can bestow upon others.

What happened on the trip to Angola wasn't the spiritual epiphany I had anticipated during this year's Lenten journey. But it was obviously the one I needed.

To Carol, Jamey, Justin, Boston, Stanton, Gary, Warden Cain, and the brothers at Angola, I'm grateful. What is happening at Angola is deserving of the widest broadcast, for what is going on there is hallowing the very ground upon which the prison rests.

The Wonders of Baseball

"Play ball!" With that sacred call to action, Major League Baseball's All-Star midsummer extravaganza will commence at our own Kauffman Stadium next Tuesday night, July 10.

Returning to Kansas City after a 39-year absence, this year's All-Star game brings to the greater Kansas City metro area a host of visitors who will enjoy an array of activities over a five-day period, July 6-10.

And for many if not most of the visitors and hometown enthusiasts, the wonders of America's pastime will dance in our hearts. The wonders of the game of baseball are multitudinous to me and include the following:

- Baseball is the single-most democratic sport of them all, because all kinds of people with all kinds of shapes and weights and heights and physiques can play it.
- Baseball is the most popular sport that isn't ruled by a clock. In some sense, you could say it has the potentiality of timelessness.
- Baseball is, as George Carlin reminded us all, the most gentle and elegant of sports, since you go to a park to see it played on a diamond. It's a pastoral game, played on a field, usually outdoors. It's always a game of new beginnings suffused with hope, commencing in the spring, the season of new life.
- Baseball is a game sensitive to the weather. If it's raining, the players come in from the field and the game is delayed.
- Baseball is a game for conversation and relaxation for spectators. There's never too much going on on the field that will interrupt a good talk with a friend.
- And, as Carlin also reminded us, baseball is a peaceful game in which the objective is to go home and be safe!

Throughout the years I've garnered many other wisdoms and insights and much saving knowledge from baseball:

1. I learned a new word from Dizzy Dean, that the past tense of slide is "slud." As in, "Did you see the cloud of dust that pea-picker kicked up when he slud into third?"

2. I learned that one could defy the normal restraints of aging and human physiology, as I beheld Nolan Ryan be a phenomenal pitcher across four decades of competition!

3. I learned how one individual can restore the trust of the American people, as when Babe Ruth virtually saved baseball after the 1919 Black Sox scandal rocked the credibility of baseball to its core.

4. I learned how one individual could contribute mightily to saving the soul of America, as I discovered how Jackie Robinson's heroic stoicism withstood the ravages of racist taunting unlike that which any other professional athlete ever faced before or since.

I hope and trust we all will enjoy the All-Star buzz — as much as we possibly can! — over the next several days!

Steeple of Light

Community's "Steeple of Light" has stimulated quite a bit of inspiration and commentary among thousands of people throughout the greater Kansas City metropolis and throughout the nation. As of this issue of the *Community Church News*, we have heard comments from as far away as California and New York, and we have received newspaper clippings from friends and associates throughout the Midwest. We have been extremely grateful for each and every one of the kind remembrances and the thoughtful enclosures.

Many of the current articles to pass across my desk have been the result of an Associated Press story and photograph that recently "went out on the wire" all across the nation. In the near future the *Historic Preservation* magazine and *Art in America* will include a story about the "Steeple of Light," and *Art News* will feature the lights in a story which is slated to run in May. We also expect to continue to receive queries and expressions of interest from the wide array of architectural associations and guilds which have already made contact with Community regarding our addition to Kansas City's night-time skyline. How long this dialogue will go on is anybody's guess. We are certain, however, that the responses to our "Steeple of Light" will not only abide but also grow in their nuances, depth of feeling, and varieties of interpretations.

The verbal communications we've received from those who have seen the lights have been unanimously positive and affirming. If I were to summarize the various sorts of statements and appreciations which have come Community's, they would fall into the following categories:

1. "The 'Steeple of Light' is simply beautiful!"
2. "Awesome! It really inspires awe!"
3. "It's truly a landmark! What a wonderful addition to Kansas City!"
4. "You know I can see Community's 'Steeple of Light' all the way from _____!" (We've had reports of sightings from as far away as KCI Airport; 126th St. and Holmes; Grandview; Lenexa; Gladstone; Independence; Kansas City, Kansas; and elsewhere.)
5. "I'm so glad Community did this! It's a historical

fulfillment, an architectural marvel, and an artistic wonder! There are few public sculptures that are as exciting as the 'Steeple of Light.'"

6. "Somehow, I feel better about the Plaza, about Kansas City, about the world, because it's there. It's a sign of hope, for sure!"

7. "How much does it cost the church to run the 'Steeple of Light?'" (To which we can say with confidence, "About $700 per year.")

The "Steeple of Light" reminds us of the great human hunger for meaning and beauty, our cherished responsibility to help satisfy that hunger, and the thrilling gifts God has implanted within and among us for the fruition and the redemption of the world.

What I've Learned While at Community (After 10 Years)

The following is a meandering compendium of observations, aphorisms, imperatives, suggestions, and musings pertaining to the knowledge I've gained and experiences I've garnered since coming to Community Christian Church. Some of these insights have sprung up like fresh, yet frightening, epiphanies. Other bits of learning have happened along the way, almost coincidentally. Still other occasions of growth have come from long-held convictions being reinforced in a new context. While this "Top 25" list doesn't exhaust the task of rumination, it does serve, I believe, as a summary of the substance of what I have proffered in prior "views" offered in this column.

- There's a place for everybody at the Lord's Table.
- Our Elders are quite often full of child-like glee, and our children are frequently full of seasoned wisdom.
- The search for peace, on any level — personal, familial, filial, professional, social, and societal — is at the heart of the religious quest.
- You can never say "Thank You" too often.
- Worship is always at the heart of the church's life, serving as the epicenter for everything we do as Christians.
- Loving service on behalf of others should always be joined to joy.
- You can try anything once. If it works, please do it again, but not just next week. If it doesn't work, please don't ever do it again.
- There is no place prettier than a Community Christian Church worship service on Christmas Eve.
- Creativity is always to be prized.
- Music is the language God uses to express the divine heart's longing.
- Love without justice is soft, and fuzzy, and mostly innocuous; justice without love is cruel, and brutish, and ultimately reptilian.

- The arts and religious experience are kissing cousins.
- The sound of children in worship is a sure sign of blessedness.
- The constant grace and tender mercies of the congregation are overwhelming and overflowing.
- Easter is one loud, long, beautiful blast of proclamation, hardly in need of embellishment.
- Do good work, pray hard, trust God, love others and oneself, and the effective responses (spiritual, institutional, relational, and otherwise) will definitely come in due time.
- Heighten your praise of all people, especially children.
- Jesus really did come "so that [our] joy might be full."
- 90% of the trick of existence is merely paying attention.
- The worst slight any human being can give others is to treat them as if they are invisible.
- Sometimes the task of a Christian is simply to believe for others when they cannot believe for themselves.
- There is a fine balance to be struck — in worship especially, but also in one's personal, family, and work life — between the need for meditative reflection and the need for exuberant celebration.
- Babe Ruth made it into the Hall of Fame as the premier baseball player of all time, and his success rate at the plate was only 34.2%.
- God loves you and there's nothing you can do about it.

The Teaching Tomatoes

As a full-blooded, unrepentant city-slicker, I don't know beans about tomatoes. But, thankfully, Priscilla does. So this year's crop of tomatoes is unlike nearly any other in any previous summer. And, even though I know more about concrete than I do about dirt (or tomatoes or arugula or snap peas or banana peppers or any other edible piece of vegetation), our little 8x 15' La Metairie patch on our home's south side is teaching some obvious lessons. And mostly, for me, the tomatoes are the instructors.

First of all, I now know what "prodigious" really means. It means you can't harvest the cherry tomatoes fast enough to keep up with their fruition. We're not going to be able to eat even one-tenth of what can be picked!

Secondly, there is pleasure, rich pleasure, deep olfactory bliss, in the sheer smell of tomatoes. If you ever need a reminder of life's unmitigated goodness, all you need to do is walk by our tomato plants. Or our neighbor's lavender hedge or our other neighbor's roses. Gardens are the original aromatherapy centers.

Thirdly, a great harvest of tomatoes is achieved when there's a grand balance of sunshine and rain. Now, I admit that this should be as obvious as the nose on my face, but remember I'm a city kind of guy, and the rhythm of sunshine's power and rain's nurturing comfort can sometimes elude us city-slickers. But this week, amidst the undulating rain-heat-rain-heat-rain-heat-rain cycles of our weather, even I can see the rate of growth among the tomato plants, their burgeoning heft weighing down the tomato cages almost to the point of collapse.

The Religion on the Line Radio Show

Information. Amusement. Entertainment. Inspiration.
Education. Encouragement. All these elements (and much, much
more) happen on the weekly radio call-in show called *Religion on
the Line* (ROL) airing every Sunday morning on KCMO 710 AM.
For nearly six years now, Rabbi Michael Zedek (senior rabbi of
Temple B'nai Jehudah), Father Thom Savage (former president
of Rockhurst College and currently with The Mercer
Corporation), and I have held forth with Kansas City's extended
family of citizens in a regular conversation about all manner of
topics, religious and otherwise.

Listeners to the show and readers here may be interested to
know that we have attained some high ratings marks in
comparison with the competition. ROL is the highest rated call-
in format show on Sunday mornings and the top KCMO show
for the day. Among all area stations, ROL is the fourth-highest
rated Sunday show overall. e have the remarkable (and sad)
distinction of being the only show of its kind in existence among
all shows on all stations in the greater Kansas City area. I say
sad, because it is our belief that such interfaith dialogue should
be more commonplace and not so rarified.

Listeners and readers may also be interested to know some
of the insights we have gained over the past half-dozen years.
These items might be termed "What We Learned at the Radio
Station."

- *Electronic media is powerful!* The reach and effect on
  people from all areas and all walks of life are
  tremendous. Not a week goes by that I don't meet —
  somehow, somewhere — someone new to me who has
  been either inspired or intrigued by the ROL
  conversation.
- *There arises a kind of cult of personality among listeners'
  expectations.* That is, there is a kind of expectation among
  our listeners — grounded apparently in the way we
  sound on the air — that we are to look a certain way,
  appear in certain kinds clothes, or even be a certain age.
  For example, to many listeners Rabbi Zedek sounds
  much taller than his physical stature actually indicates.

For another example, our listeners often assume, and rightly so, that we three enjoy each other's company and laugh a lot; they say they can hear the smiles in the voices

- *One talks faster on radio than in normal conversation.* It is amazing how rapid-fire our delivery can become. This is so, I suppose, because of the time constraints of the radio program itself. The ROL conversation is time-bound and segmented into quarter-hour chunks. There are paying customers (i.e., sponsors) to honor and PSAs (public service announcements) to insert. And we normally feel a great urgency to include as much information as possible in response to listeners' questions and comments. The radio format is excited by speed and pace, and appeals to only one of the senses, sound. Thus, all movement, texture, depth, and dramatic dynamics are related to the various ways that sound can be shaped, changed, and made interesting. This isn't a conscious effort on our part, but rather something that has developed organically over time.

- *Wondrous (and life-changing) events of pastoral care can and do take place even when people only meet as voices on a radio show.* A young woman mourning the death of her grandmother after she prayed for her release from cancer. An older woman seeking guidance about how she might best approach her own imminent death. A man's wistful longing for a community of welcome. The struggles of a person suffering under the burdens of oppressive fundamentalism. The strivings of a heretofore irreligious person seeking guidance about the best sort of scared literature to read. All this and so much, much more can transform ROL into an occasion of sacramental encounter some Sundays.

- Principles of inclusion, acceptance, and most importantly, a celebration of the wondrous diversity of religious experience are finding a greater resonance within the embrace of more and more folks. And nothing could make us feel more gratified than this achievement thus far.

I'm extremely grateful for the possibilities ROL provides so many people. We'll continue on until we get it right, or at least until we get better and better. We are thankful for the enthusiastic support of our countless listeners and participants who call in. Whether on the radio airwaves, or in this column, or in the context of worship, I'm always very glad to greet you.

The Biggest Little Word

Most of the great words of Christian faith can be uttered in single syllables. Look at Jesus' most famous and familiar declarations, The Sermon on the Mount, and you will behold small bundles of words that pack a tremendous wallop. View Jesus' Galilean ministry, hear his call to the twelve apostles, witness his journey to Jerusalem, and you will always notice how powerfully straightforward and amazingly unpretentious he was.

Nearly all great personages throughout history traffic in uniquely simple notions and profoundly uncomplicated ideas.

Plato's genius vocabulary runs persistently toward the piercing truth of simplicity.

Churchill's great clarion call to the British people to endure entailed no great rush of polysyllabic pabulum, but rather focused on the need for "blood, toil, tears, and sweat."

In one of the most inspiring addresses in recorded oratorical history, Abraham Lincoln stunned his admiring listeners at Gettysburg with a mere 267 words.

And we can never forget the searing vision of Mother Teresa in our own time, or the lightning-like power of Sojourner Truth from a time gone by: in these two women profound and proud truths issued effortlessly and simply from their lips.

Over and over again, we know with ever-clearer insights the plain and obvious reality: truth, particularly religious truth, comes unadorned, in simple garb.

Now, not yet two weeks after our exciting and exultant Easter Sunday celebrations, we are called to focus on Jesus' simple ways. And what are they? Faith? Hope? Love? Peace? Forgiveness? Loyalty? Yes, but there is more.

There is one simple word which Jesus used again and again in his earthly ministry and which he used in his communing with the disciples. It is a simple word which deserves our special attention each and every day, but especially right after Easter. It is contained in Jesus' Great Commission at the conclusion of Matthew's gospel. What is the biggest little word?... "Go!"

Rowing

Recently, I started a new venture: rowing. Answering an ad I saw on The Dime Store shop window in the middle of our Brookside neighborhood one hot July evening, I signed up for several weeks of instruction on the verities one could learn and the vitality one could experience strapped into a 42-foot-long, five-person rowing boat. It has been a wonderful endeavor, though troublesome at times. Full of fantasies of rowing down Brush Creek — an impossibility, I now realize — or cruising up and down the Kansas or Missouri Rivers — now a lived reality — I've come to have an awakening with regard to the painful particularities of learning anything from scratch.

First, there is the vocabulary. Words and phrases like "gunnels," "starboard," and "way enough" are now part of my ready-to-use lexicon. ("Way enough" is my current favorite new rowing word, but requires far more space to explain than this column allows.) It's invigorating to learn fresh new words about a new subject in a new learning context.

Next is the equipment, all of which is provided by the KC Rowing Club. My, my, my! I never knew such boats cost as much as they do — and weigh as much — as I've recently found out. (Somehow, the cost of those beautiful sleek water-slicers we see every four years during the Olympics, or every so often in movies like *River Wild*, never even occurred to me. And because they traverse the water's surface with seeming effortlessness, like feathers sliding over glass, I always imagined, heretofore, these sorts of boats weighed nothing.)

Perhaps best of all, the crew of 5-7 of us who gather early on dewy Saturday mornings for our rowing classes have quickly discovered that any efficient and satisfying rowing experience depends on proper preparation. Each and every time we get together, the boat has to be lugged approximately one hundred yards, carefully up and over and down the levee by the Kansas River behind the stockyards. (On a hot day, it seems much longer, steeper, and several sweaty T-shirts more difficult!) Then the boat must be properly positioned in the water and outfitted with the right accompanying gear. Then comes the hardest prep work of all — inside our heads and throughout our muscle memory — as we struggle to coordinate at least 17 different individual and collective actions and reactions in order to move the boat forward without tipping it and drowning ourselves in the process.

Regarding this last reference to the universal concept of "teamwork," I've learned all over again an adage that family, church, school, and life-in-general have continuously impressed upon me: it really doesn't matter what clothes you wear, but it ultimately does matter what attitude you bear. Our attitude toward the task of rowing itself, toward each other as novice crew mates, toward the boat and its undeniable and tangible realities, and toward the waters we traverse, always determine the quality of our time together as newly learning rowers. Whenever everything is good — when the boat is rightly trimmed and we catch our strokes in a common rhythm and the sun is glinting on the water and our attitude is of one, peaceful, strong accord — rowing is a thing of beauty and wonder. And at times like that I assume I am not alone in thinking, in some small corner of the mind, that surely we could at least come in third in Atlanta next summer.

Obviously, or so it seems to me, there are some parallels between rowing and the Church: we are always learning or re-learning the vocabulary of faith and the lexicon of love; proper equipment (such as a willing spirit, a seeking mind, and one's physical presence) is necessary for the life of faith; attitude is everything; and coordinated teamwork exerted for a worthy common purpose is a beloved event to behold. What more is there to say but . . . "Row, row, row, your boat!"

New Year's Resolutions 2014

1. I will indulge myself, and I will encourage others to indulge themselves, in the gatherings and the graces and the lasting gifts of life: meals shared with those we treasure, love expressed as often as we can, an abiding focus on what makes for justice and goodness for all, walking as humbly as we can, day by day, knowing that God wants us, all of us, all of God's children, to enjoy life to the hilt.

2. I will give all that I have, and I will give it freely. I will not hoard or save or stockpile — for a later time or a better date — any compliment, poem, idea, notion, support for a worthy cause, any laugh, any hug when hugs are wanted and needed.[1] I will eagerly seek out and be open to the insights and gracings of others. I will rise to the challenging question: Why should any one of us be lost if someone else knows the way?[2]

3. I will spend what I don't have, that is, that which I so much enjoy and treasure but of which I can never claim sole ownership. I will share God's love that comes to us all freely and generously, a gift never to be possessed solely by any one person but is a universal spiritual currency.

4. I will let my heart be broken, broken open to a world in need of caring and hope. I am not an automaton but a human being, and so I will maintain a bruisable heart, a vulnerable center of my personality, a capacity to be affected by the world and all of its inhabitants.

5. I will attend to the needs of children, never failing, so far

---

[1] See Annie Dillard's *Give It All, Give It Now: One of the Few Things I Know About Writing* (New York: Welcome Books, 2009).

[2] See Samuel Green's poem *"Postcard: 10/18/01, NY,"* *The Only Time We Have: New Poems* (SedroWoolley: Grey Spider Press, 2002), p. 37, which is also included as "Oct. 18 New York City," in The Grace of Necessity (Pittsburgh, Pennsylvania: Carnegie Mellon University Press, 2008).

as I can help it, to receive happily a greeting from any child and then return it with enthusiastic appreciation. I will remember that all children — in this congregation, in this city, or any other — are our children.

6. I will forego violence in my language, in my actions, and, of equal importance, in my assumptions and my attitudes toward what the world brings to my door, even if what it brings is chock-full of violence.

7. I will nurture and care for three specific bodies: my own, for it is the only vehicle I have for negotiating life through this world; the body of the earth, which is the carrier vehicle for the entire human race; and the body of the faithful that gathers here, for it needs my efforts, my prayers, my support, if it is going to be hale, hearty, and healthy as a witness for good in the community and in the world.

8. I will smile at the world as often as I possibly can, sometimes through clenched teeth, to be sure, but knowing that negativity never has worked and only a glad heart can live a fulfilled life.

9. I will take in as many movies as I can and listen to as much music as I can and behold as much visual art as I can and witness as many performances as I can and read as many books as I can, for the splendors of human creativity are sheer gifts and glimpses of the divine.

10. I will be as truly human and humane and alive as I can muster, and live my days with attention and engagement, and not simply visit this world. As Mary Oliver puts it succinctly, about this year or any other.[1]

(These resolutions were shared during the New Year's Welcoming Service at Community Christian Church, Kansas City, Missouri, on December 31, 2013.)

---

[1] See Mary Oliver, "*When Death Comes,*" **New and Selected Poems** (Boston: Beacon Press, 1992), p. 11.

Religion On the Line — Celebrating 20 Years On the Air!

The Sunday morning broadcast of the live, weekly radio call-in show *Religion on the Line* on KCMO 710 AM/103.7 FM will observe its 20th anniversary in May. When the show began, Rabbi Zedek, Fr. Thom Savage, and I had no idea that the program would have such longevity.

Some statistics about the show tell an interesting tale:

- **Number of shows broadcast:** 1,000+
- **Number of studio locations:** 3 (in the Manor Square Building in Westport) , 1 (in Westwood), and the current location (in the Mission Bank building).
- **Number of Catholic hosts as part of the ROL crew:** 5 (Fr. Thom Savage of blessed memory (1993-1997), former President of Rockhurst University; Fr. Pat Rush (1999-2000), Vicar General of the Catholic Diocese of Kansas City-St. Joseph; George Noonan (2001-2007), Chancellor of the Diocese of Kansas City-St. Joseph; Fr. John Wandless (2007-2008), Diocesan priest; and Dr. John Purk (2008-present), Catholic deacon.
- **Number of Jewish hosts:** 1 (Rabbi Michael Zedek, Rabbi of Congregation Emanuel Chicago, Illinois).
- **Number of Protestant hosts:** 1 (Bob Hill).
- **Number of guest participants**: approximately 150, ranging from seminary interns to local clergy to national commentators to international dignitaries.
- **Number of station owners during ROL's time on the air**: 3 (Bonneville Communications, Susquehanna Communications, and Cumulus).
- **Increase in commercials and news breaks per show**: From 7 per broadcast (in 1993) to 11 per broadcast (in 2003) to 40 per broadcast (in 2013).
- **Number of calls in 20 years**: approximately 30,000.
- **Number of commercials**: 40,000+.

Mother's Day

The U.S. observance of Mother's Day began with Anna Jarvis, who, in 1858, wanted to heighten awareness about the health conditions in her community in Appalachia. Originally the day was called "Mother's Work Day," and was envisioned also by Mrs. Jarvis' daughter, also named Anna, who began a campaign to honor the work of her mother and to lobby politicians to set aside at least one day dedicated to the country's mothers.

In 1872, Julia Ward Howe, author of the words to the classic "Battle Hymn of the Republic," proposed a "Mother's Day for Peace" which would be an annual commemoration in service of abolishing war. The first church service organized with a Mother's Day emphasis occurred in 1908, with carnations being passed out to those in attendance.

In 1913, the U.S. House of Representatives approved a resolution calling for elected federal officials to don white carnations on the second Sunday in May. On May 8, 1914, President Woodrow Wilson signed a resolution officially designating the second Sunday in May as Mother's Day, as "a public expression of our love and reverence for the mothers of our country."

Since that historic commencement, Mother's Day has been attached to many movements and causes. (Recall "Another Mother for Peace" and "Mothers Against Drunk Driving.")

In the Christian faith, the impact of Mary upon Jesus cannot be overestimated. And there is no doubting the significance of women in the life and ministry of Jesus and in the development of the Church.

Trying to think of Christianity without mothers in particular and women in general would be like trying to imagine wind without air, bread without flour, a horizon without sky.

Women were the first evangelists about Jesus' resurrection. It was in the living room of a woman named Lydia that the church was birthed on European soil.

And it has been women — poor, wealthy, and in-between, insiders and outsiders, young and old — who have borne the Church in their hearts and on their backs down the long line of its development and even into our time.

Who can ever forget the women who led in every suffrage and liberation movement, the guidance of wise women in the doing of mercy and justice, the teaching and tutelage we gained from Sunday School teachers, the life-saving works of sewing circles and women's auxiliaries, the searing vision of one like Mother Teresa, the unwavering courage of one like Joan of Arc, the lightning-like power of one like Sojourner Truth? And how could we ever forget the impact of women in the life and heritage of Community Christian Church?

At Community, Mother's Day Sunday will not only be a day for sentiment, but an opportunity to express our deepest affection and appreciation to those who gave us life and to honor the legacy of all women at Community who have been and are fonts of nurture, care, and wisdom.

Mothers' Days

While the official observance of Mother's Day is certainly a venerable high point in the middle of May, we need not throw all of our affirmation onto just one day. There are plenty of other occasions and instances of "mothering" realities in our shared culture.

Mother cells duplicate themselves rapidly. *Mother courage* is very important to character development in every individual. However we measure patriotism, we all possess a sense of rootedness in our *mother country*, and we all can and should claim the need for prudent stewardship of *Mother Earth*.

House mothers provide care and guidance for countless members of sororities and fraternities, just as *mother houses* offer abiding places of nurture, instruction, and spiritual formation for those following religious paths, often led by *mother superiors*.

Important popular mother figures have influenced us, fictional and real, including the likes of *Mother Hubbard, Mother Goose,* and *Mother Theresa*. We must admit, though, that few of these can help much when it comes to fixing a computer *motherboard*.

One can easily grow weary of those who hover like *mother hens*, but we become nostalgic and downright homesick for the sound of our *mother tongue*. And while it seems beyond doubt that necessity is often the *mother of invention*, it is an absolute certainty that there is no pearl without *mother-of-pearl*. And one's access to and sustenance from *mother wit* can seem like *mother's milk* and/or like hitting the *mother lode*.

It just may be, given all this mothering, that all days may rightly be called Mother's Day!

As we approach this year's special day of sentiment and proverbial wisdom, we should not forget the ancient Jewish proverb which affirms what children know instinctively: "God could not be everywhere, and therefore God made mothers."

Rodin and "The Sufficiency of the Fragment"

In the latter part of the 19th century and into the earliest part of the 20th century, Auguste Rodin revolutionized the art of sculpture and what it can mean for the world. As his artistic star rose, he was deemed the greatest sculptor since Michelangelo.

The Nelson-Atkins Museum in Kansas City currently has a stunningly wonderful exhibit of Rodin's works — *RODIN: Sculptures from the Iris and B. Gerald Cantor Foundation* — and you would do yourself a big favor by exploring and enjoying it at your earliest convenience.

Beyond our familiarity with Rodin's famous pieces like "The Kiss" and "The Thinker," a version of which sits on the Nelson's grounds, there are untold numbers of Rodin's other sculptures that deserve our attention and appreciation. Those who have been to the Museé Rodin in Paris will attest to the grand scope of Rodin's genius.

In the current exhibit here in our own backyard, there is an abundant array of the master artist's work. Among the pieces in the current assemblage, and especially toward the end of the exhibit, there are some small figures and fragments of Rodin's sculptures. Throughout Rodin's career such figures and fragments were intentionally set apart as singular, standalone works of art, even as they were crafted in anticipation of larger endeavors.

The museum commentaries attached to these smaller pieces describe Rodin's belief in "the self-sufficiency of the fragment." By that he meant that a part could and can stand for the whole. A portion of a body has integrity in and of itself and can represent the entirety of the body. An arm can express the complete grace of a courageous gesture. A torso alone can define the overarching anguish of one despairing. One hand by itself can reach for the whole world.

Jesus taught this, and we know and believe this to be true as people of faith. We are not the creators of "the light of the world," but we are graced vessels for it. None of us can reflect the entirety of the light of God's love, for we are, in more ways than we can ever imagine, only fragments of that light. But there is a "sufficiency in the fragment."

God has chosen each and every one of our lights to shine forth in the darkness. As the promise was secure for Christ's light — "and the darkness did not overcome it..." — so, too, is that same promise sure for us as well. So, let it shine. It is an exceedingly good thing to do. And it is and will be a beautiful thing to see, now and for the ages.

Love on Valentine's Day

While not a church holy day in very many circles, Valentine's Day does have church roots. The myths about "St. Valentine" are many and varied.

Among the most popular recollections is one about a valiant Christian named Valentinus, who was jailed because of his steadfast refusal to venerate any of the Roman idols during the reign of emperor Claudius II Gothicus. The jailer's daughter, Julia, so the story goes, came and visited Valentinus, and he tutored her in mathematics and faith in God. Blind since birth, Julia received a note from Valentinus at the time of his execution, February 14th. The note thanked her for her kindness during his imprisonment and was signed "Love, from your Valentine."

As the story also goes, when Julia received the note, her sight was restored. The year was 270. The gate where Valentinus was executed was later named Porta Valentini in his memory. It is said that Julia herself planted a pink-blossomed almond tree near his grave at what is now the Church of Praxedes. Because of the reported miracle of Julia's restored sight and the compelling power of Valentinus' faithful witness, Pope Gelasius I of the Roman Catholic Church eventually, in the year 496, decreed February 14th as Saint Valentine's Day.

A millennium and a half later, we are now fully engaged in remembering St. Valentine's Day, though, in the U.S. context, with a lot more chocolate than when it began.

Over the years traditions have multiplied. In Wales carved wooden "love spoons," with hearts, keys and keyholes as favorite decorations, were given as gifts ; the decorations meant, "You unlock my heart."

In the Middle Ages, young men and women would draw names from a bowl and then wear them on their sleeves for a week. In contemporary times, chocolate sales soar, flower orders quadruple, restaurant reservations triple, and marriage proposals and weddings abound on Valentine's Day, as on no other day on the calendar.

It's all good, in my book. I encourage us all to enjoy the day as much as possible with as much enthusiasm (and chocolate) as we can muster. And let us also honor the occasion's inspiration, which no mythology can confuse or obliterate: love.

With regard to love, allow me to suggest three actions for your consideration:

1. Say your love to those closest to you. No matter how often or infrequent you may normally say it, engage in the practice of verbal love with those in your innermost circle of relationships.
2. Pray that love may be infused in all relationships, in all aspects of human existence. From the meagerest to the mightiest person on the face of the globe, love is the ultimate mold in which we were all created. Love is our origin and our destiny, and we cannot be fulfilled until we experience love in all of its fullness.
3. Live in such a manner that the work of love will be increased worldwide and help to defuse international crises. Love is not merely kind words on a card nor only a nice sentiment expressed one day of the year. Love is an ethic for the living of our days. Jesus mandated love as the key to our relationships with God, neighbors, and even enemies. The apostle Paul described love's enduring capabilities when he correctly noted that "Love never ends."

In the long run, hate can never prevail in human relationships. It is only the ethic of love that can build a better world. It just may be that a keener appreciation for Valentine's Day could be an ultimate blessing for the world's future.

Leaves from The Notebook of A Tamed Optimist

Once, while preparing a talk for a seminary group regarding ministry in general and preaching in particular, I was reminded of Reinhold Niebuhr's great book *Leaves from the Notebook of a Tamed Cynic*. Inspired by Neibuhr's fetching title but much different in my basic attitude toward life, I fashioned *20 Leaves from the Notebook of a (Barely) Tamed Optimist*. I should add that the talk was guided by some wisdom from an array of colleagues, friends, and revered teachers from around the country. The subjects in this wonderfully random and sociologically airtight survey came from four dozen or so people, including: one seminary president; three faculty members from three different seminaries; two social service agency leaders; two regional ministers; six clergy colleagues in Kansas City; eight lay-people; one Fred Craddock (what category do you put Fred in? He *is* a category!); and two pastor developers. The advice from the informal survey I conducted rendered some gems of good guidance:

"Just tell them to read. Just read."

"Express your creativity."

"Understanding human experience is the first and foremost, the primary, undertaking of the clergy."

"They — we — all of us need to hear some good news."

"Hang on to hope."

Aided by advice and supported by suggestions, I went on to proffer ten brief leaves from the notebook of a (barely) tamed optimist. While space doesn't permit me to share the full extent of the leaves, I would offer the following ten, not only for ministers, but for Christians as a whole, especially those who share our faith in and through Community Christian Church.

1. *Whatever one proclaims, whether in word or deed, do so with some passion.* (And that doesn't just mean more volume. When John Wesley was asked why people came to hear him preach, he could only say, "I really don't know. All I know is that the Spirit sets me on fire, and people come to watch me burn.")

2. *Know what you believe and tell folks your absolutes.*

3. *How one presents the gospel is crucially important.* (In other words, presentation sometimes can indeed be everything.)
4. *Develop an expertise in something that you are good at.*
5. *Let the music flow.* (In our public and private lives, music is an elixir.)
6. *Cultivate a discussion about preaching and worship with one another.*
7. *Analyze institutions in light of post-modernity.* (What does it mean to be church in a culture that doesn't regard institutions as valuable?)
8. *Being attentive, not merely being available, is what pastoral care is about.*
9. *Take care of yourselves.* (Rabbi Ed Friedman's wisdom is always salient and on the mark: "As a leader goes, so goes your congregation.")
10. *Relationships are key.* (We were made for relationships and are not fulfilled until our relationships are fulfilled.)

Give Them, Give Them All, Give Them Now!

One of Annie Dillard's best books, *Give It All, Give It Now*, a book I've quoted from in sermons before, consists of only 122 words. Actually, the text is from one of her earlier books, *The Writing Life*. Despite the book's brevity, the wisdoms in *Give It All, Give It Now*, and the illustrations that illuminate them, are astonishing.

As we move through the valley of the shadow of the tragedy at Newtown, Connecticut, and as we approach ever closer to the gift of Christ's birth at Christmas, I think Dillard's words are worth remembering and repeating. In fact, I believe they have some saving graces for all of us this year.

"One of the things I know about writing is this: spend it all, … play it, … all, right away, every time." Dillard goes on to say that "the impulse to keep to yourself what you have learned is not only shameful, it is destructive. Anything you do not give freely and abundantly is lost to you. You open your safe and find ashes."

As with writing, so with the gifts we give at Christmas time. Events like the horror that descended on the people of Newtown and the suffusing sadness that has spread throughout all of the country call us to be as generous as we possibly can with the best gifts we have for one another: faith, hope, love, joy, peace, cherishing honor, structuring our lives in ways so that further such tragedies are avoided, tender listening, warm embracing, comforting support, caring compassion, seeing our own tears in another's eyes, sacred laughter.

Dillard also goes on to warn about the dangers of refraining from giving our gifts: "Do not hoard what seems good for a later place in the book, or for another book; give it, give it all, give it now. The impulse to save something good for a better place later is the signal to spend it now. Something more will arise for later, something better. These things fill from behind, from beneath, like well water."

Again, as with writing, so with the best gifts we give at Christmas. The gist of the Christmas story is this: God did not hoard the birth of Christ for a better place later or for another world or another time. And neither should we. In the loving gift of Christ, God gave it all and continue to gives it all now, in our time, as well.

So, this year, this Christmas season, let us all share and sing and tell everyone about the gift of God's love — wherever we are, wherever we go — along with the other best gifts we know — faith, hope, love, joy, peace, cherishing honor, — structuring our lives in ways so that further tragedies are avoided, tender listening, warm embracing, comforting support, caring compassion, seeing our own tears in another's eyes, sacred laughter. Give them, give them all, give them now!

For the Beauty of the Earth

Among the messages we always hope to transmit to our
children, one of our premier concerns surely has to do with our
mutual care for and enjoyment of the natural world. From
recycling centers to EPA regulations, from the impressive
expanse of a city park to your own back yard, from the top of the
stratosphere to the deepest chasm of the ocean, care for the
earth's ecology is paramount. Earth Day should and can be more
than one shining moment in the spring. As I see it, the lessons
we teach children about the earth and its great entrustment to us
are similar to those timeless truths we offer children about life in
general.

1. **Love your mother!** We all want our children to love
    their parents, and of course, in special ways, to uniquely
    love their mothers. So it is also with the earth. It
    behooves us all to teach all children a caring, endearing
    love of Mother Earth. Earth, like a human mother, gives
    life, gives sustenance, gives hope. By loving Mother
    Earth, we offer the best care we know, not only for the
    physical world but for ourselves who live within it.

2. **Respect and be proud of your home!** Given this early
    instruction by parents, aunts, uncles and grandparents,
    I've been subsequently inspired toward activities like
    keeping a relatively straight house, mowing the yard
    with great vigor, despising the sight of a stray piece of
    paper in an out-of-the-way place, and more. Likewise,
    with the Earth, let us respect and be proud of our global
    home. Just think what might transpire if we were to treat
    the entire earth as we would the favorite area of our
    homes, apartments, yards, and farms.

3. **Remember where you came from!** Location and locale
    are intrinsic components to one's identity. None of us
    are from nowhere, nor can any one of us be from
    everywhere. We all hail from someplace, and
    remembering our places of origin helps us understand
    who we are, what we are to do, and how we are to
    conduct our lives. So it is with our relationship with the

earth. We are all made from earthy substances. To put it like the ancient prayer does: "... earth to earth, ashes to ashes, and dust to dust." And if we remember that we come, in large part, from rich, earthy stuff, we will treat the earth and each other with a greater honor and a kinder appreciation.

For Our Veterans on Veterans Day

On this national holiday, I'm sending warm greetings and affirmations to all veterans and veterans' families among Community's members and friends — and indeed to all American veterans everywhere — who have given sacrificially for the shared values and civic dreams we prize above all others: freedom, justice, and equality for all.

My favorite lines in "America the Beautiful" are in the second verse: "O beautiful for heroes proved/ in liberating strife,/ who more than self their country loved,/ and mercy more than life." While many can lay claim to that sentiment, our veterans are among the chief patriots "who more than self their country loved."

During my lifetime, America's military service personnel have been engaged in one "conflict" or "war" or "skirmish" or "initiative" after another. Our veterans have answered the call whenever it has been issued, and we have witnessed their valor at every turn. That we have not discovered better ways to resolve international differences and global tensions is a commentary on a lack of political will and imagination, and there is much work to do on that front. But our veterans and the families of our veterans have been exemplary in sacrifice, steadfastness and determination. And for that we say "Thank You" once again.

A good friend who served several tours in Vietnam once expressed utter humility and hope in one simple statement, and I haven't forgotten it: "I just did my duty. One day we'll figure out better methods of dealing with things than shooting at each other." May we all increase in our sense of duty and our hopefulness for a better world.

First and Last Words

The yearning to communicate — through the blossoming of a real linguistic expression or the rumble of some language-like sounds — is born within us. We rejoice when it becomes expressed at the beginning of life. And we treasure beyond measure the occasions when we witness it at the end.

Parents can attest to those cherished moments when a child utters a "first word." What joy there is when a child says "Mama" or "Dada" or some variation thereof. Sometimes a child's "first word" is an unexpected word, like "car," or "Jello," or "baseball." No matter the actual word, each is sacred.

Likewise, family members and friends will attest to the holy moments when "last words" are heard. There are umpteen collections of "Famous Last Words," and they nearly always manage to amuse, charm, and inspire. Regarding these benedictory moments, I am sure Steve Jobs' last words will be anthologized in most of the forthcoming versions of such books.

Approaching the end of his life at the too-early age of 56, Jobs died, like all human beings die, *in medias res* (into the middle of things), saddening countless admirers and the general public that his genius would no longer grace the waiting world with his inventions and creativity.

Still, despite the premature nature of his passing, which was preceded by a long battle with pancreatic cancer, Jobs uttered a profound final acclamation: "Oh wow. Oh wow. Oh wow." What he saw or heard or felt at the end of his earthly journey abides in mystery. But his last words were an excellent summation of how he encountered the world and how the world received the fruition of his creativity. "Oh wow. Oh wow. Oh wow." Good "last words," indeed.

Whatever our first words may be, may we live such lives that our last words will be kind and caring and generous, and perhaps even as exuberant as those Steve Jobs declared at the end.

Famous

The word "famous" has two basic definitions: (1) widely known and honored for great achievement, and (2) excellent and first-rate.

Recently, Community was associated with a person who is clearly connected with the first definition. Word spread pretty rapidly last week when Al Roker of *The Today Show* was shooting his national NBC weather forecast near the J.C. Nichols fountain with Community's building in the background. Kirby Gould, whose office is in our Activities Center, even had her picture taken with him. Facebook friends gave Community happy shout-outs. There was some enjoyable buzz about Community's proximity to such a celebrity.

Of course, every congregation can point to famous persons who have graced their buildings and their histories. Among the famous personages who have graced Community throughout our history are Jane Addams, Peter Ainslie, Edward Scribner Ames, Marian Anderson, Forrest Church, William Sloane Coffin, Bob Costas, Fred Craddock, Clarence Darrow, W.E.B. DuBois, Dale Eldred, Millard Fuller, Toyohiko Kagawa, Anne Lamott, Sinclair Lewis, Vachel Lindsay, Edwin Markham, David McCullough, Karl Menninger, Reinhold Niebuhr, Buck O'Neil, Charles Sheldon, John Shelby Spong, Noel Paul Stookey, Doc Watson, and, of course, Frank Lloyd Wright. But there is more.

This is where the second definition of famous comes in to play. Community's recent brush with Al Roker got me to thinking about the truly famous people who are connected with Community's family of faith week-in and week-out.

The attitude of caring to one and all by Community's members and staff is ultimately far more significant than our architecture.

The acts of kindness in times of crisis, to strangers and friends alike, by Community's faithful are more meaningful than any of the meaningful things stated by the potentates and pacesetters who have spoken from our chancel.

Endeavors for justice and service by those who congregate at 46th and Main St. are better measures of our involvement in transforming the city and the world than who has spoken about those concerns in our venue.

The devotion and prayers of Community's family of faith, individually every day and in weekly corporate worship, are more beautiful and powerful than any artistic expression by renowned professionals who visit our facilities.

And what goes for Community goes for every other congregation as well. The ultimately "famous" are in the midst of those who gather for worship, service, study, and fellowship every week.

Awash in a celebrity culture, we're unlikely to evade some excitement when folks like Al Roker come to town. But may such occasions serve a higher purpose, namely, to remind us of the truly famous already among us.

Ministry

Every Christian is called to participate in ministry in his or her life. Day in and day out, we are all engaged in what the Protestant Reformers called the "priesthood of all believers." This is a mutual ministry which all people possess within the church.

Whether clergy or laity, ministry has many definitions. Just consider the following:

Ministry is a cup of cold water to the parched soul. It is a shining beacon of hope to those struggling in desperately dark straits. It is, to paraphrase D.T. Niles, simply one beggar telling another beggar where to get bread.

Ministry is the refreshing wind of good news to the stolid personality who had feared that there was no inspiriting wind at all. It is a comforting shoulder to lean on, to cry on, to stand upon. It is the quieting forgiveness offered to one haunted by phantoms of guilt.

Ministry is the nod of acceptance and affirmation when everyone else is flippant and we direly need to be taken seriously. It is the laugh of comic relief when we take ourselves too seriously.

Ministry is the prophet's challenge when we are "at ease in Zion." It is sterling style and "real class" in the face of squalor. It is devotion to God at the expense of material gain.

Ministry is humility when tempted by status or position or unfair advantage. It is a "menu" of prayer, wherein "breakfast" is a cry for help, and "lunch" is a shout of thanks, and "dinner" is the pronouncement of "Amen!" It is God's call in the small hours of the night, when no one seems to be there but you know One is surely there.

Ministry is that to which one is called, into which one is immersed, and by which we are all tempered. It is the vista of a better world, within and without, for oneself and for all others, after long hours of meditation and contemplation. It is bread being broken — for you, for me, for all! — and the taste of the cup.

Ministry is the preaching of the Word, and the hearing of the Word, and the caring, daring, and sharing of the Word. It is the constant conjugation of God's ultimate verb, "Love."

Ministry is "comforting the afflicted and afflicting the comfortable." It is the surefire knowledge that "the opposite of love is not hate but indifference." It is teaching the yearning mind and stimulating the seeking heart.

Ministry is a hand to hold when going down treacherous steps. It is an arm to embrace when springing up from the waters of baptism. It is a blessing upon wedding rings and a benediction at the final end of one's days.

Ministry is tears shed in anguish and anger when tender ones are bruised. It is a prayer of hope in the hospital waiting room. It is the clarion call to resistance and freedom for all who would brave the barricades.

Ministry is a warm touch and a loving handshake on Sunday morning. It is being an ambassador for Christ, a messenger of reconciliation, a steward of the mysteries of God.

Ministry is a means of grace, for the sake of grace, in constant moments of grace, which are, hopefully, full of grace. It is pronouncing "Grace!" over everything.

Encountering God's Beautiful World Anew

The goodness of God's grace abounds in the world around us! As we approach the official beginning of summer, the earth is flourishing with wonderful new growth. Grass, shrubs, bushes, and luxuriant lawns are resplendently green, as green as I've seen in a long, long time, this deep into June. And gardens are gloriously plush nearly everywhere you look.

What's a proper response to all this glory? What are we to do with such incontrovertible evidence of God's generosity? What shall we do with this splendor that makes Kansas City one of the most beautiful spots in the whole wide world? The following suggestions might be ripe for consideration:

Perhaps awe-filled wonderment is simply enough, in and of itself. Most of us would benefit immensely from taking more time not only to "smell the roses" but simply to behold, appreciate, and affirm the great revelation that roses truly are. Awe-filled wonderment is what human beings are made for. A treasured hymn says it best when it describes how we are often "lost in wonder, love and praise."

But there is surely more. Perhaps we can understand awe-inspiring beauty as a sign of the immensity of God's creative powers. We revel in what we can see and taste and touch and hear and smell in the world in all of its immediacy, without filtering, censoring, or obstacle. But attending only to what our senses tell us about the external world may short-circuit the overall fullness of what God is communicating to us on a daily basis.

To put it another way, as linguist George Lakoff used to say, the world around us is "a metaphor we live by." Consider the beauty of a flower or an evergreen or a sunrise or a bird in flight. All such beauty points to the beauty of holiness which God intends for the whole world. An overwhelming thunderhead, a glowing sky at dusk, the large fireworks of a lightning storm, or the small firework of a lightning bug — all these are symbols of God's overarching creative powers throughout the universe. The awesomeness of nature is merely a sprout of God's divine intentions for all creation, including all human beings.

Which leads to yet another way that the wondrous aspects of

God's awe-inspiring world are at work. Perhaps the beauty, the power, the grace of the world are ultimately parables of God's powerful presence at work in our interior worlds. When Jesus spoke about lilies in the field and birds in the air, surely he meant to spur his followers into an examination of God's tremendous loving care for the human family, premier among all of God's creatures.

Surely God is at work in us incessantly — to empower our individual and collective patterns of growth, to activate beauty and wonder in the midst of our thinking, dreaming, praying, speaking, listening, loving, and living. How appropriate then, when we face such blessedness, that our wonder goes on and on and on. To wonder at God's grace at work in our lives is not to wander into abstraction but, quite the opposite, to abide in the true, holy image in which we were created.

As the greenest spring turns into a prodigious summer, let us remember:

1. stay awestruck about nature;
2. behold the entire universe, beyond the world as we immediately know it; and
3. consider the "worlds" within you, which God means to make whole, holy, and more and more beautiful.

Death's Sting

"The sting of death is sin?"

There are at least two ways of looking at the apostle Paul's theological flourish toward the end of his first epistle to the church at Corinth (1 Cor. 15:56).

Some folks focus on a traditional interpretation — based on their reading of the first four chapters of Genesis — that one of the ultimate consequences of sin is death, virtually inverting the positions of the words in the scripture to read, "The sting of sin is death." Taken too literally, this can connote profound guilt for any and all experiences of death, tragic or natural, including the imputing of recrimination even upon innocent victims. And countless souls know the mercy that death can be and has been for their loved ones at the end of grueling, debilitating battles with disease.

In contrast, taking the phrase metaphorically, one can easily affirm that in death there can be and often is a sting — regret, embarrassment, sorrowfulness, remorsefulness, humiliation — because of past unresolved misdeeds, errors, or offenses against others. One can certainly sense such stings long before one draws one's last breath.

Paul's overarching proclamation in the 15th chapter of Corinthians is a layered testimony, not an irrefutable template for understanding what happens when we die. He mixes his earnest anticipation of Christ's second coming with his whirling understandings of what happens to our bodies after death and his trust in God's provision of immortality.

In the end, trusting in God, and not our own worthiness, causes us to know the veracity of what Paul will declare just a few verses later: "in the Lord your labor is not in vain."

Still another way of putting this is to remember the bard Bob Dylan's insight: "He not busy being born is busy dying." We are called to the grace of being born again and again and again through God's love, which can assuage any sting.

(This is the original version of a piece that appeared in a Voices of Faith column for *The Kansas City Star*, January 17 2015, in response to the question, "What does the Bible mean when it says: 'the sting of death is sin?'")

Back to the Garden

A phrase from an old song has new meaning for me these days, more than two generations after the song captured the essence of a musical festival held near Bethel, New York: "...and we've got to get back to the garden."

The garden in the song was an idealized, imagined place, and it echoed the Bible's first garden. There are other songs and tunes galore extolling the glories of returning to such an edenic scene.

One can easily suppose that there is in all of us a sighing after Eden. That's William Willimon's description of our human yearning to revisit a presumed pristine state of innocence and freshness.

But that's not a garden I or anyone else can ever get back to. What we can do instead is go forward and find again, or maybe for the first time, gardens in our own backyards.

A trip this summer to Johnny and Deborrah Wray's High Hope Farm in Cedar Bluff, Mississippi, inspired a new focus on gardens, farms, and food. While my visit to Johnny and Deb's acreage was brief, it was a revelation. Their creative combination of technology and natural pasture makes it possible for cattle (about 12 head), chickens (about 700 egg layers, 600 meat chickens), turkeys (225) and pigs (60) to coexist in a symbiotic balance, reducing the extra fertilizer they have to buy and increasing the health of their livestock and the healthfulness their livestock will render for those of us who will enjoy them at our dinner tables. And their fruitfulness is simply awesome. (I had never heard of Mumbo Jumbo as an egg size!)

Now, of course, I'm never going to be a farmer, nor a rancher for that matter. My soul is soaked with too much love for cities for me ever to switch to a preference for the rural over the urban. Still, despite a lifelong allegiance to cities and city life, certain words are now gaining considerable purchase in my heart, head, and soul. Words like land and rain and growth and gain and manure and sustainability and preserving and putting by.

Priscilla has enjoyed a close acquaintance with such realities for quite a while. Attaining the status of Master Gardener over the years, she has overseen the maturing of La Metairie (Little Farm) on the south side of our home. Delectables like tomatoes, peppers, green beans, snow peas, scallions, beets, okra, collard greens, arugula, and lettuce have blessed our table and our lives during bounteous summer months. And when the harvest has waned and occasionally withered — because of drought or a pesky fungus or marauding assaults by squirrels and rabbits — we ponder the largesse and the losses, the boon and the bane, the giveth-and-taketh-away character of creation.

The difference in me since visiting High Hope Farm is that I now believe such an acquaintance is a necessity for all of us, if we want to live fully, and with greater health and vitality, into the deeper reaches of the 21st century. The trip to the Wray's thirty-acre farm prompted in me a new awareness of Eden's contemporary correlatives.

Eden is not merely a back-when, then-and-there place or predicament located only in Genesis. Rather, it's the humble patch to be found in your own backyard and the rolling expanse of a municipal park and the small-scale farm yielding healthier food and naturally nurtured livestock. In the end it's the entire planet we call home. The air and the water and the dirt that make food possible are not small matters but huge aspects of what it means to live a fully engaged life.

It was a delight to share in the bounty of Johnny and Deb's farm, as dinner one night included okra, beans, corn, tomatoes, scallions, and peaches, all from their land and made possible by their hands' labors. And it's been an intriguing return to life in Kansas City as I've paid more attention to food (and its origins), whether in a restaurant or at home. It just may be I'm doing as the old song urged us to do.

Just after the visit at High Hope Farm, I heard the sad news that legendary Texas writer John Graves had died. He will be forever remembered for his first (and best) book *Goodbye to a River*, now regarded as a classic (not unlike Thoreau's *Walden*) and a staple in college English courses. This summer I'm saying "Hello" to a garden.

Always Building

All of God's creatures are always building something.

Beavers build dams.
Bees build hives.
Ants build anthills.
Rabbits build warrens.
Lions build dens.
Birds build nests.

So it is, too, that the building instinct runs rampant among human creatures as well.

Bricklayers build walls.
Construction workers build skyscrapers.
Carpenters build houses.
Woodworkers build cabinets.
Salespeople build client lists.
Guitar players build chords.
Doctors build practices.
Composers build symphonies.
Conductors build orchestras.
Orchestras build crescendos.
Power-seekers build reputations.
Sculptors build sculptures.
Autoworkers build cars.
Ship-builders build boats.
Lawyers build cases.
Bankers build fund balances.
Politicians build campaigns and campaign treasure chests.
Elected officials build legislation.
College presidents build campuses, student bodies, and faculties.
Gardeners build compost piles.
Olympic committee participants build stadiums and arenas.
Astronomers build telescopes.
Opticians and optometrists build eyeglass lenses.
And parents build families.

Yes, we are all of us about the activity of building in one way or another.

In the realm of faith the building motif continues. In church activities our concern is to build, assemble, fashion, establish, shape, form, create, erect, make, and otherwise construct a meaningful spiritual life.

This matrix of significant events builds us up individually and communally, so that we can be, as the book of Ephesians puts it, "built together spiritually into a dwelling place for God."

A Wondrous and Happy Mess

Recently my friend Seymour dropped by my study at Community and exclaimed, "Whoa! What happened here?"

I brought Seymour up to speed about the new carpeting being installed throughout the church and that my study was one of the first offices to be redone. I told him how the good folks from a local moving and storage company had moved all of the books, bookcases, furniture and files in my study out into the church's art gallery area. I recounted how the carpeting people installed the new carpet, and then the moving people put all the bookcases, books, furniture and files back in place.

"I must say, the carpet, at least the portion I can see, looks great!" Seymour observed. "But what happened to your books?"

I responded by telling him that the books had all been put back, just not in the places I had previously placed them.

"Uh-oh!" Seymour mused. "Makes it difficult to find certain books when you need to consult, review or read them," I suspect.

I agreed with Seymour but also said that it offered a great adventure of rediscovering books long overlooked and that it was stirring me to cull books I know I'll never return to.

"All in all, I've got a wondrous and happy mess on my hands," I admitted to Seymour. And I'm alerting you, too. If you drop by church to see me in my study, please excuse the mess. The new carpet really is beautiful under all the books.

You Are Welcome!

One of the apostle Paul's greatest sayings is found in his letter to the church at Rome: "Therefore, since we are justified by grace, we have peace with God." Or, put another way, God has rolled out the "Welcome" mat of grace for us. We have been made right with God, set in right relation with the divine. In still other words, God is saying to humanity, "You are welcome in this world."

And while it may sound rather plain, pronouncing "You are welcome!" with warmth, hospitality, and graciousness is one of the highest callings of Christians.

In the face of the crustiness of the world, the vitriol too often spewed in our media, and our culture's too-frequent inclination toward the negative, we all yearn for a sense of welcome in the world. Theologian Paul Tillich once described how we are all looking for the experience of being accepted, and that God provides it. He declared God's unalloyed welcoming commitment to humanity in very simple terms: "You are accepted."

"You are accepted." "You are welcome." Such grand and beautiful gifts.

One of the best gifts we can give to another person is to say, "You are welcome." You are welcome here in this life. You are welcome in this your own dwelling place. You are welcome in your own skin. You need not be any other person or abide in any other location. Here and now, you are justified, you are accepted, you are welcome.

May we be more and more a place and a people of welcome, and may we be more fully so each and every Sunday in our "concrete tent" of a building at 46th and Main St., and indeed wherever we find ourselves out and about in the community.

ACKNOWKLEDGEMENTS

It is almost impossible to express my fullest gratitude to everyone involved in bringing this book to fruition, but I must try.

For the constant and unfailing encouragement in writing and in life, I'm thankful to Priscilla, first critic, best appreciator, the one who is truly "the best."

For personal support along the way and wise guidance to the kind confines of Woodneath Press, warm thanks to Brent Schondelmeyer, friend and writer extraordinaire.

For the cool, calm and collected editorial oversight of Cody Croan, augmented by the enthusiastic affirmations of Steve Potter and Andie Paloutzian, a deep sigh of smiling thankfulness is in order.

And for the grand, glorious congregation of Community Christian Church, "a church in the heart of the city that takes the welfare of the city to heart," my undying love for taking me into your heart. It was among you that most of these words were first shared.

ABOUT THE AUTHOR

Robert Lee Hill served for more than 30 years at the Community Christian Church (Disciples of Christ) in Kansas City, Missouri, before retiring and being named minister emeritus in 2015. Prior to arriving at Community, he served for four-and-a-half years as Special Projects Director and Co-Director of Project Return, Inc., a non-profit agency working with ex-prisoners and their families in Nashville, Tennessee. He holds a B.A. degree from Texas Christian University, an M.Div. degree from Vanderbilt University Divinity School, and a D.D. degree from Christian Theological Seminary. Since 1993, he has been co-host of the renowned Sunday morning radio call-in show *Religion on the Line* on KCMO 710 AM/103.7 FM. He has written or edited eight other books, including most recently *The Color of Sabbath*.